With Best Wishes
Swaha Sellamuthu

Book Layout & Design by:
Ideagram Communications Pvt. Ltd., Chennai

Cover Design by:
Andrew Neill

Printers:
Aitken Spence Printing & Packaging (Pvt) Ltd,
Mawaramandiya, Sri Lanka.

Before it's all forgotten

A collection of recipes encompassing tradition and creativity...

Before it's all forgotten

A collection of recipes encompassing tradition and creativity...

Author

Shivahari Sellamuttu

Dedication

The most high God I praise you. Without you, this book would not have been possible for me. From the day I found you, you blessed the work of my hands, lifted me up on high and helped me in all my ways. Whatever I have asked you have delivered and I know you will make all crooked places straight, for you gave me this promise, and guided me as I wrote this book. Glory is to God.

This book is dedicated to my children Sunny, Natasha and Johann who have shared with me three generations of recipes. In the kitchen and at our dining table, each of these recipes evokes special stories of loved ones past and present. My family and I have laughed and wept reminiscing about tales of our family history. We continue to enjoy these dishes and in turn we are creating more beautiful stories for generations to come.

Shivahari Sellamuttu, 2012

Acknowledgement

I would like to thank all the people who assisted me with editing this book. Among them are Andrew and Natalie Betts, and Ramona Nizar.

I would love to thank Pam Fernando, Sheryl Fonseka for allowing me to cook in their kitchens and to be able to shoot pictures in their beautiful homes.

To my friends Sriyani Tidball, Sheryl Jinasena, Romola Sivasundram and Dihan Inman for their advice and encouragement that made me believe that I could make this book happen.

To my best friend Eva Gubcsi, thank you for all the endless advice, support and encouragement you have given me.

I would also like to thank my sister Ramani and her husband Vikram Thambuswamy, for the support and suggestions they offered in order to help me enhance this book.

To my children, grandchildren, and Sherwin, this book would not have been possible without your love, support and for believing in me. I love you all dearly.

Finally, thank you to my mother Nahamma, Aachie, Putti Aachie, Aunty Naheswari and all the cooks and chefs who have inspired and shaped my love and passion for cooking.

Book cover is an abstract painting done by Andrew Neill.

Food Photographs: Nizar Mohamed, Soli Nizar, Pino Uganotti, Prashan Subramaniam, and Neil Abeynaiyke. Many thanks for your patience and help to make this happen.

Scenic pictures: by Sandun de Silva. Thanks for taking the time to travel to the northern district to take colourful images for my book

FOREWORD

My main credential for writing this foreword is that I have a passion for cooking, adore food and all things food related and over the years I have spent many a deeply satisfying afternoons or evenings enjoying Shivahari's unique style of cooking and her generous hospitality. Although I grew up in the same country as Shivahari, it was through her cooking that I was first introduced to a range of flavours and foods that I hadn't tasted before.

Shivahari grew up in Colombo, the capital of Sri Lanka. She spent her school holidays with her grandmother, in their ancestral home in the ancient northern city of Jaffna. This region is well known for its abundance of seafood and a range of fruits and vegetables not found in any other part of the island. The food here was developed over centuries by people with an immense love of food. So at an early age Shivahari was introduced to the specialities of this region; to pickles, achars, chutneys, curries, soups, snacks and sweets that were unique to the north. She spent hours walking through the food markets of Jaffna with her grandmother, marvelling at the displays of enticing fresh produce, whilst the family cooks trailed behind, their shopping.

When she wasn't playing hide-and-seek in the palmyrah groves with her siblings and neighbourhood friends, her favourite past-time was to sit on a low wooden stool in the family kitchen and watch her grandmother's cooks as they stirred pots of steaming curries, chopped strange looking herbs and ground pyramids of spices in readiness for the day's meals.

The cooks plied her with a constant supply of tasty 'treats', which was encouragement enough for Shivahari to linger, absorb the aromas and build on her food memory bank. The care and love that went into their cooking inspired her and awakened in her an interest in cookery that eventually led to her own career in food. Since 1971, the year Shivahari first arrived in Australia, she has been preoccupied with cooking. For several years she ran her own highly successful restaurant in Melbourne called SHIVAHARI'S. Following the sale of her restaurant, she worked as resident chef in several other popular restaurants in Melbourne and Sydney, until she finally turned her culinary expertise to private catering. Her cooking methods are simple and her easy to follow instructions are written with the novice cook in mind.

There is no one better qualified to introduce us to the flavours of the northern region of Sri Lanka than Shivahari. The variety of the cuisine of northern Sri Lanka, as showcased in this book, has not been captured in a recipe book before. In this book Shivahari has successfully linked through her recipes the simplicity of the past with the complexity of the present.

This book is a must if you want to try recipes that take you off the culinary beaten track and lead you on a journey of exploration into the complex flavours of Sri Lankan food. Each dish reflects the many external cultural influences that have created the food of the Sri Lankan people and some of the recipes are unknown outside the area in which they originated. This book also contains new versions of old favourites.

Shivahari believes that cooking is the heritage of any family and sharing her recipes ensures that these unique dishes are never lost to the future generations. Many of these recipes have been scrawled on little bits of paper and pasted in worn out exercise books or passed from one generation to the next by word of mouth. However, she knows that in today's fast-paced era, unless these traditional family-style recipes are recorded, they will disappear forever.

I hope that Before It's All Forgotten, as well as being used as a cookery book, will be a book to treasure and pass on to the next generation.

Diane Inman
Sydney, 2012

TABLE OF CONTENTS

TABLE OF CONTENTS

TABLE OF CONTENTS

Introduction

Introduction

I am so happy to be meeting you through the pages of my special recipe book. These recipes that I share with you here represent the stories of so many experiences of my life. They are reborn, to be shared with you, in this very book. Each recipe comes from a different space in time. They form a collection of exotic tastes to bring to your dinner table and to share with your loved ones and friends, just as I have. Historically, some dishes have been in my family for many generations. Many special people in my life have prepared these dishes for me, in their colourful and busy kitchens. Some recipes I have personally developed from my many years of cooking professionally and preparing food for my family and friends. Cooking is my life, as it represents a creative vessel through which I can express my love, happiness and other emotions that sometimes may be hard to be expressed in other ways. Those who know me well know that each dish I prepare is created with hope, love and passion.

Cooking is a very personal and individual journey. I can say to you that my experiences of cooking have seen times of hardship, which grew into strength and hope. At other times they were filled with joy, laughter and even solace. No matter what, cooking has always been a voice to be heard and a way to hear others. I would like very much to share my journey with you by cooking, and sharing with you some of the stories and history of these recipes. I hope that each dish you prepare is filled with hope, love and passion and manifests a precious story of its very own in your kitchen or at your dining table to be enjoyed and endeared for generations to come.

Background

My family heritage extends to my Tamilian cultural background, which is strongly influenced by Northern Sri Lankan and South Indian provincial foods. Although my cooking is diverse, the dishes from these provinces are special to me as they have been handed down to me by my grandparents, my mother, my aunties and the very special cooks we had in our homes. I always get excited when preparing these dishes; they evoke so many fond memories from my childhood to the present day. I see these dishes as the legacy of my departed loved ones and the legacy I wish to instill in my family today. The important meaning behind the strong connection of three generations of traditional recipes can continue by sharing these recipes with you. I grew up in a very large family. I not only lived with my parents and siblings, but also with my grandparents 'Patta' and 'Aachie', my father's parents. Food always brought us together, particularly the times I shared with my mother and her mother, my Aachie. My mother would often speak about my great grandmother, her father's mother, who lived with them from the time she was a young girl. Whenever my mum cooked any beautiful Jaffna specials she would talk about 'Putti Aachie' who made beautiful authentic curries. I was fascinated the way she spoke of her grandma and her lovely curry combinations that I had not heard of or eaten before. She says that she had a style of her own, and was very creative. I enjoyed cooking at home, and for celebrations, and as I grew older I knew in my heart that one day I would take after my great grandmother with the same passion and love for food and for the pure experience of cooking. This is the very reason I took to cooking as a career. My early career in cooking began when I migrated to Australia in the 1970s, where I went into partnership and started a restaurant called 'Shivahari's' in Melbourne. My namesake restaurant served authentic Sri Lankan cuisine derived from the recipes handed down to me by my mother, grandmother and other family members. My mother often helped me with the business by sharing these recipes and old traditions and ideas of Sri Lankan food. Throughout the years I made my home in Sydney where I worked in many restaurants such as 'Radio Cairo', 'The Sri Lankan Room', 'The Curry Connection', 'Botanical Gardens' and 'Maharajah's' to name just a few. I had a major setback when I suffered serious injuries to my knees at work and I was no longer able to work as chef. This was a serious challenge and obstacle in my life as cooking was such a huge part of me, and my life. However, with the encouragement of my family and friends to pursue writing this book, the passion within has been re-ignited. To hear my family and friends say how my food brings them joy and happiness gives me a sense of personal fulfillment. To share the dialogues of my ancestors through the preparation and tastes of the recipes in this book comforts me, knowing that these dishes and stories have a chance to be heard again before it is all lost. I hope that you will enjoy our journey together through these pages where you will see that the one vital ingredient to cooking is passion.

My Paternal Grandparents

The weather was so humid but when it poured it was fun. I loved to run in the rain just singing and dancing. I would have all the younger ones following my routine. We would all be drenched and shivering, but just having fun. My Patta had a long cane woven seat that he would sit on relaxing and watching what we kids were doing. On this particular day, Patta had asked the domestics who worked at that time to call us inside. Cyril, Modesta and Kusuma were all calling out to us to come inside, but we chose to ignore them. My Patta became very annoyed. He had a cane in his hand and I knew we were in real trouble. Trying to escape Patta's smacks, I remember darting across to the bathroom for a shower, saying I had to get in the shower before I caught a cold. Oh boy was I in trouble! Patta was such a distinguished man who loved us so dearly. Aachie, on the other hand, was a very sweet quiet person who sat at this long head of table all day giving instructions to all domestics from the cook, gardener and driver. It was a big household. Both Patta and Aachie took care of all our needs and loved us dearly. My father had passed away when I was 9 years old. There are many stories to tell, but they will come later in another edition hopefully. By the time I was thirteen years old both my grandparents had passed away. I have beautiful memories of my grandparents that I will treasure for the rest of my days.

Adigar Arumugam Sellamuttu

Thaiyalnayaki

My Maternal Grandparents

When we were kids we would travel to Jaffna on the slow overnight train called Yal Devi. My maternal grandfather, Karalasingham, chaperoned my cousins Radha, Shiva and my sister Ramani and I. His caretaker, Kandan and his wife Annapillai used to do all the cooking. In the olden days there was no running tap water. At the back of this beautiful country style home was a large garden. I remember walking through this beautiful garden adorned with a variety of Jasmine, hibiscus, lime, mango, pomegranates, margosa, jackfruit, drumstick and king coconut trees. I was an early riser. The sun rose early and it was so humid at that time of the morning. I enjoyed having my early morning bath at the well side and I would walk up to the large well where Annapillai would be waiting to draw water from the well for me to have my bath. I remember sitting on square granite stone in my swimsuit, while Annapillai would pour buckets of refreshing cool water over me. Ramani and my cousins would join later one by one to have their baths. We had such a great time. The climate was always sticky and hot, and we all enjoyed the freshness of the well water on our backs!

Annapillai was an amazing cook. She would make many of the Northern country style dishes, and I would spend time in the kitchen just watching her and asking her questions about the spices, and why each spice had a different texture. The spices, whether they were fresh or dry-roasted, were formed into golf-ball-size for everyday cooking. When I was growing up in this country style home, the kitchen was very simple. No gas stove or electric hot plates. Instead there was a cook-top built from clay, and they used firewood for cooking. All cooking was done in iron wok skillets and clay pots. It is the same kitchen that my great-grandmother, Ponnamma, cooked in with the help of Annapillai when she was a young girl.

Karalasingham

Bahirathy

My Recollection Of Jaffna By Shivahari

After our tedious journey from Colombo, back to school in Jaffna, I couldn't wait to go to the town centre. Better still if it rained, as it enabled me and my friends to stomp on muddy potholes on the road. I vividly recollect bullock carts, transporting bags and boxes of rice, grains, spices etc. In those days there were no organisations against animal cruelty. I also remember the market place where Tamil and Sinhala traders from Galle and Matara, the Deep South and Muslim regions (traders who mainly controlled the beef, chicken and mutton stalls) would live alongside harmoniously. The Sinhala and Hindu Tamils even prayed at the same temple, due to the closeness shared between Hinduism and Buddhism.

In the town, the rich people would show off their Morris Oxfords, Austin Cambridge and Wolsley motor cars. The best of the British buildings were the colonial ones like the Post Office, Kacherie (Government Offices), library and other buildings, constructed in typical Dutch and English architecture. The Catholic Churches were built of Portuguese artistic design.

I remember during Deepavali (the festival of lights) my grandparents, cousins, my siblings, the driver and I would get crammed inside our Austin A40 when we go for sightseeing. Now I wonder how the driver got to see the windscreen through us kids. To be honest, we were more interested in the sweet-meats served at our relatives and friend's home rather than the religious implications. The firecrackers, joss sticks and the aromatic

incense added another dimension to these festivities. As a young ten year old, I used to think, "If only this festival of lights could last longer." However, I used to enjoy the love, joy and happiness that everyone around gave me. I had my share of solace by accepting the fact that Deepavali, the beautiful festival of lights, will be back again next year. Life was slow and I am sure the saying, "Don't do today what can be done tomorrow" originated in Jaffna. The food of Jaffna has never been documented in a comprehensive way, nor is there a complete account of generational family recipes such as those passed down by my mother to me. The cuisine of this region has an extraordinary range of flavours and interesting ingredients that grow only in specific regions of Sri Lanka. Through my recipes I want to reveal the Sri Lankan cuisine and culture that needs to be preserved. Hot climate, rich soils, islands of exotic fruits and spices—it is no wonder that Sri Lanka has developed a reputation for some of the tastiest curries in the world.

Due to lack of rainfall, the soil here was very arid. Our fathers and forefathers have put in their blood, sweat and tears to cultivate this land and nurture this soil with their tender care (This I bet was more than their wives got!!).
Be it the giant trees like Mango, Jackfruit, Coconut and Palmyra trees or the ground hugging herbs and spices, all these are the outcome of their hard work and dedication. The quality and taste of fruits and vegetables here is simply amazing. The nectar of Jaffna mango is arguably the worlds finest. For decades (even now) no artificial fertilizers are used in growing them.

The unpolluted waters of the Indian Ocean around Jaffna, produces some of the finest seafood. Due to traditional line fishing the eco balance is still maintained. The fishmonger would bring to us the freshest of fishes, mud crabs, succulent king prawns, kanaeva (squid) and different species of small fishes from the many mangroves in Jaffna. The sight of this array tantalized our taste buds so much that we kids would get impatient waiting for the finished product for our lunch or dinner.

To my many readers who would visit the beautiful island of Sri Lanka, do take out your time to visit Jaffna and see the natural beauty of this place. The pristine greenery and scenic beauty of this place is so pure and pleasurable that it is a sheer bliss to wake up to everyday!

Appetisers, Soups & Drinks

The Yal Devi train was a slow train, to Jaffna. My sister Ramani and I went to school at Vembadi Girls High School which was an elite girl's school. We did our school leaving certificate in Jaffna.

I was always sad to leave because I knew I was not coming back to the city until the term ended, so there were many tears leaving behind a loved one but soon my friends would make me laugh and I was over it. Going back to boarding school, after the holidays we caught the night train which was a slow train. It stopped at all stations and it was steamy and exhausting. My friends and I had so much to talk about, especially about how we had spent our holidays, and then we would have a singsong and play games. I remember when we stopped at some country town stations there were vendors selling spicy gram with pieces of fresh coconut made from chick peas, potato bondas, masala vadais, ulundu vadais with chutney, spiced cardamom tea, and hot kappe (coffee) and they would run towards the train as it was pulling up to the station to get a sale. The fond memories inspired me learn how to make these delicious snacks.

Masala Vada

Masala Vadai

INGREDIENTS

3 cups chana dhal (yellow split peas)
1 cup water
2 medium white onions OR Spanish onions, finely chopped
1 sprig fresh curry leaves, finely chopped
6 green chillies, finely chopped
¼ cup plain flour
1 teaspoon chilli powder
½ teaspoon black peppercorns, coarsely cracked
2 tablespoons salt
Sunflower oil for frying

METHOD

Pre-soak chana dhal for 3 hours, then wash thoroughly under running water until clear and drain.

Using a food processor, grind chana dhal gradually with ½ cup of water. (Don't add too much water, as the paste has to be fairly thick.)

Add flour, and remaining water and continue to grind until it is a soft dough.

Place mixture in a bowl and fold in the chopped onions, peppercorns, green chillies, fresh curry leaves, spices and salt to taste.

Meanwhile, heat oil in a deep frying pan over a moderate heat.

Shape dough into 2–3 cm balls and then slightly flatten them to form patties.

Deep-fry them in oil until crisp.

Allow them to drain on absorbent paper and serve hot or cold.

Masala Vadai is best served with Green or Red Coconut Chutney

Potato Bonda

Potato Bonda

INGREDIENTS (POTATO MIXTURE)

500 g Pontiac potatoes (if unavailable any other potatoes can be used)
1 medium white onion OR Spanish onion, finely diced
2.5 cm piece ginger, ground
3 green chillies, finely chopped
1 sprig fresh curry leaves
1 teaspoon chilli powder
1 teaspoon turmeric
½ cup fresh coriander leaves, finely chopped
1 teaspoon black mustard seeds
Sunflower oil for frying

INGREDIENTS (BATTER)

2 cups besan flour (chickpea flour)
1 teaspoon baking powder
½ cup cold water
Salt to taste

METHOD

Peel and cut potatoes into cubes then place them in a pan of water and boil until soft. Drain well and roughly mash potatoes and set aside.

Heat vegetable oil in a wok and fry the onion until golden and add green chillies, ginger, fresh curry leaves and mustard seeds sauté until aromatic.

Next add chilli, turmeric powder and salt to taste and stir.

Finally, add cooked potatoes and fold through spices adding chopped coriander leaves set aside. Allow potato mixture to cool.

In a mixing bowl combine chickpea flour, baking powder, and salt to taste and gradually stir in water to make a fairly thick batter. Set aside.

Place oil in a deep frying pan and heat on medium to high heat.

Place heaped tablespoons of the spiced potato mixture in the palm of your hand and shape into small balls.

Dip potato balls in prepared batter to coat well, and drop them in the hot oil, fry until golden brown.

Potato Bondas are delicious when served with Mint Chutney.

Raal Appam ~ Prawn Cutlets

Raal Appam ~ Prawn Cutlets

INGREDIENTS

500 g King Prawns, de-veined and shelled
1 medium red onion OR white onion, finely chopped
4 cloves garlic, finely chopped
1 sprig fresh curry leaves
1 teaspoon chilli powder
1 cup grated fresh coconut OR desiccated coconut
2 teaspoons fennel powder
1 teaspoon cumin powder
1 teaspoon black peppercorns
1 egg, lightly beaten
Salt to taste
2 tablespoons of oil
Sunflower oil for frying

METHOD

Heat oil in a heavy base pan.

Add prawns and sauté over a low heat, adding chilli powder and salt until prawns are cooked (about 8 minutes).

Drain juices from the prawns and allow to cool.

Place fennel seeds, cumin seeds and black peppercorns into a small frying pan and dry-roast over a medium heat until golden and aromatic. Set aside.

Place coconut, curry leaves, dry-roasted spices and garlic in a food processor and blend to form thick dough.

Add chopped onions to the cooled prawns and continue to blend on low speed until mixture is coarse.

Remove mixture from food processor place in a glass bowl, and fold in beaten egg to form a glossy –dough texture.

Heat oil in a deep frying pan over a medium heat and place 1½ tablespoon portions of the mixture in the palm of your hand and shape into balls.

Thumb press lightly and place in heated oil and fry until golden.

This dish is best served with Pudina Chutney.

My mind is full of wonderful things; times I have loved and shared with my sister and brothers. Deep in my mind is love; the love and care we have shared with each other-the happy times at St Edwin's, my dad's father's home where we all grew up. This home was a seven-bedroom home in Cinnamon Gardens, with a front garden big enough to have a cricket field. We would play matches for fun with our cousins or with our neighbourhood friends. My favourite time of the year was the rainy season. It would just rain in the middle of the day. I loved the thunder and lightning and remember Kandiah's Pan Rolls and Roll Cutlets with Chilli Sauce. For some reason he always made these yummy dishes for dinner and we would have them with steamed vegetables or homemade chips.

Roll Cutlets

Roll Cutlets

INGREDIENTS (FILLING)

500 g lamb OR beef (ground)
750 g potatoes (Golden Delight OR Pontiac)
300 g white onions, finely chopped
10 green chillies, finely chopped
1 teaspoon chilli powder
1 sprig fresh curry leaves
2 ripe tomatoes, finely diced
2.5 cm stick cinnamon
6 cardamom pods
3 cloves
2 tablespoons black peppercorns (coarsely ground)
2 tablespoons vegetable oil
1 tablespoon butter
2 tablespoons roasted curry powder
2 tablespoons Worcestershire sauce
2 tablespoons white vinegar
Salt to taste

INGREDIENTS (EGGWASH)

6 eggs, lightly beaten
Breadcrumbs
Sunflower oil for frying

METHOD

Wash potatoes, place in a pan of salted water and boil until cooked.

Drain, cool and peel. Mash thoroughly until smooth and fluffy (the potato mash must be like a dough like consistency and pliable).

Add 1 tablespoon of butter to potato mash mix. Set aside while you begin to prepare the filling.

Marinate ground meat, in a glass bowl with coarsely ground peppercorns, salt, curry powder, Worcestershire sauce and vinegar and mix through. Set aside.

In a large saucepan, heat oil over on medium heat and onions sauté till golden, next add green chillies ,curry leaves and tomatoes, and cook mixture until it thickens.

Then add the ground meat and spice mixture and stir through, continuously until meat becomes separated and moisture is completely absorbed.

Set aside and allow it to cool.

METHOD (RISSOLES)

Rub a little olive oil into the palm of your hands and place 2 heaped tablespoons of the mash into the palm of your hand to form a round ball.

With your thumb make an indent in the ball of mash, large enough to fill with meat mixture.

Fill potato ball with 1 heaped tablespoon of meat mixture.

Use the remaining potato to cover meat mixture and mould into elongated croquettes (roll cutlets). Place on a flat tray.

Repeat this step until potato mash and meat mixture is finished and place in the fridge for 1 hour.

In a glass bowl beat the 6 eggs to make an egg wash and set aside.

Place breadcrumbs into a deep bowl.

Generously coat the roll cutlets in egg wash and dip in breadcrumbs.

Repeat this step until all roll cutlets are crumbed and chill for 30 minutes.

Deep-fry the roll cutlets in oil until golden.

This dish is lovely with Chilli Mayonnaise.

Beef Pan Rolls

Beef Pan Rolls

INGREDIENTS (BATTER)

2½ cups plain flour
3 cups cold water
4 eggs
½ teaspoon salt

INGREDIENTS (MEAT FILLING)

500 g premium quality beef mince
1 tablespoon Worcestershire sauce
1 medium white onion, finely chopped
2 tablespoons dark roasted curry powder
1 tablespoon soya sauce
1 sprig fresh curry leaves
4 medium potatoes, peeled, boiled and
mashed roughly
1 teaspoon cracked pepper
Salt to taste
1 tablespoon vegetable oil
Sunflower oil for deep-frying

INGREDIENTS (EGG WASH)

4 eggs, lightly beaten
2 cups water
½ cup plain flour
Breadcrumbs

METHOD

For the batter, use an electric mixer and beat eggs, flour, and water to make a smooth batter.

Add salt and set aside while preparing the meat mixture.

Heat oil in medium saucepan, add onion and fry until golden.

Add fresh curry leaves, meat and fry until brown.

Add sauces, curry powder, salt and cracked pepper and cook until almost dry, adding the mashed potatoes and salt to taste.

Cook for further 5 minutes. Cool.

Pour 2 tablespoons of batter into a 22 cm non-stick frying pan and cook over a medium heat.

Cool on flat surface and repeat till you are out of batter.

Place on flat surface and fill each one with 1 heaped tablespoon of meat filling.

Wrap into small packages by bringing the two sides together and then roll one side firmly to resemble a spring roll set aside.

To make the egg wash, whisk eggs lightly in a mixing bowl and add water and flour to make a fairly thin batter.

Dip pan rolls into combined egg wash mixture, and then roll them in bread crumbs.

Cover and refrigerate until ready to use.

Deep-fry pan rolls in hot oil until golden and crispy. Drain on absorbent paper. These are great as a finger food at any party. Serve with Chilli Mayonnaise.

Ulundu Vadai

Ulundu Vadai

INGREDIENTS

3 cups Urid dhal (black gram flour),
available from Asian supermarkets
2 medium-size onions, finely chopped
1 teaspoon ginger, freshly grounded
6 green chillies, chopped
1 sprig fresh curry leaves, crushed
2½ teaspoons salt
1 teaspoon water
Sunflower oil for frying

METHOD

Pre-soak the Urid dhal for 4–5 hours.

Drain dhal and grind ⅓ of the dhal with 1 tablespoon of water in a food processor or grinder.

Repeat the process until all the Urid dhal is ground. (The mixture should be coarsely ground).

Transfer mixture into a large bowl.

Add finely chopped onions, green chillies, crushed curry leaves, ground ginger and salt to taste. Set aside.

Meanwhile, heat oil in a deep frying pan, over a medium to high heat.

Place 1½ tablespoons of ground mixture in the palm of your hand and shape into 2–3 cm rounds.

Lightly flatten and make a small incision in the centre to resemble a doughnut.

Gently drop into hot oil and deep-fry until golden brown.

Serve with Green or Red Coconut Chutney.

I want to thank my very dear special friend Sheryl Jinasena and her Cook, Mahinda for sharing a delightful mouth-watering Ellai Kangi recipe that I was lucky enough to have enjoyed when I was on holiday in Sri Lanka. We had it for breakfast like porridge with a side dish of Hakkuru (Palm Sugar). I have taken it to another level by serving it as a soup. Its rich flavours remind me a lot of a Kangi we had while growing up. Instead of using dried spices, I like to prepare it with the freshest ingredients, including fresh coriander, continental parsley, mint and English spinach. Watercress can be substituted if the leafy vegetables are not available. Mahinda's version is beautiful but many of the ingredients aren't available outside of Sri Lanka, therefore I experimented with all the beautiful exotic herbs and greens when I made it for my family. Mahinda has someone to help him wash various herbs and greens as required. They have to be blended. The coconut is scraped and the milk has to be extracted for the Kangi. The process he uses is time-consuming. Back home he has plenty of help! To make things easier for people living outside Sri Lanka and wanting to cook this beautiful mouth-watering dish, I have changed the recipe around. I use a food processor to help get the job done, and use canned coconut milk. This Kola Kanda Soup is flavoursome, and has a delectable spicy aroma when all herbs come together.

Ellai Kangi (Leafy Porridge)

Ellai Kangi (Leafy Porridge)

INGREDIENTS

2 bunches watercress OR English spinach
12 sprigs fresh curry leaves
1 bunch coriander leaves
1 bunch mint leaves
½ cup fresh coconut, grated
1½ cups thick coconut milk
6 cloves of garlic, finely chopped
1 teaspoon peppercorns, finely grounded
1 cup red rice OR 1 cup long grain rice, boiled
12 cups water
Salt and cracked pepper to taste

METHOD

Wash green leafy vegetables and herbs, drain and chop all leaves coarsely.

Using a food processor, purée all the leafy vegetables and herbs with 3 cups of water until smooth.

Place mixture into a bowl and set aside.

In a blender, add the grated coconut to 3 cups of water and blend until smooth.

Strain coconut mixture through a sieve into a bowl, and place back into blender.

Add the green leafy mixture, blending again with 2 cups of water until smooth. Strain again through a sieve and set aside.

In a heavy base saucepan, add the strained mixture and remaining 4 cups of water and bring to boil over a low to medium heat.

Reduce heat to low, add garlic and boiled rice and gently stir.

Allow to cook until it reaches a smooth and thick consistency.

Add cracked pepper and salt to taste and allow to cool.

Place Ellai Kangi (soup) in a food processor and blend until smooth and creamy.

When ready to serve, simmer over low heat and gradually stir in coconut milk.

NB: Instead of fresh coconut milk substitute with tinned coconut milk.

Annapillai's Kool Soup was a special treat and it was planned days ahead. It was a late Sunday afternoon special. An elderly lady clad in a cotton sari with a woven cane basket on her head laden with various types of beautiful seafood would come by with fresh blue swimmer crabs, green prawns, squid, and fish that had been freshly caught. She would walk down the street shouting out to the neighbourhood and calling out by name the varieties of seafood she had to offer. Annapillai was always quick to get to the gate so that she got the pride of the catch. I would hear her bargaining and getting a good deal. She had already prepared the young jackfruit, chilli paste, spices, long beans and other ingredients she needed for the soup. The root of the Palmyra is dried and used to thicken the soup. I can still picture the huge clay pot with the wood fire burning. I would watch her meticulously prepare this awesome meal. It seemed like ages before the pot came to the table. She would always place the soup on a plaited coaster made from dried Palmyra leaves. We were quick to thrust the bowls at her. The soup was very hot and spicy, and I remember how my eyes would water, and my tongue would burn. Instead of using soup spoons, the leaves of the jackfruit were pinned together and used as spoons. This is a Northern Sri Lankan traditional and wholesome soup that is a meal on its own. Kool is beautifully perfumed and flavoursome, and is enjoyed by many in the Northern territory of Sri Lanka. It is very similar to the French Bouillabaisse.

Kool Soup

Kool Soup

INGREDIENTS

4 litres water
500g medium green prawns, de-veined
1 kg red Mullet fish, cut into cubes
1 fish head for the stock
½ kg squid tubes cut into rings
1 kg blue Swimmer crab, or use soft shell crabs broken
into bite-size pieces (use the shell for stock)
1 bunch long green beans (snake beans),
diced into 2.5 cm pieces
1 bunch English spinach, chopped coarsely
1 cup long grain rice
10 dried chillies with seeds
Chilli powder to taste
1 teaspoon turmeric powder
2 sprigs fresh curry leaves
3 teaspoons coriander seeds
2 teaspoons cumin seeds
1 teaspoon black pepper coarsely ground
250 g young jackfruit (fresh jackfruit is available from
Asian supermarkets)
1 large Spanish onion OR white onion
4 cloves garlic, ground to a fine paste
2.5 cm piece fresh ginger, ground to a fine paste
1 tablespoon tamarind pulp
3 tablespoons Palmyra root soaked in 4 cups of cold water
Salt to taste

METHOD

Peel and de-vein prawns, and cut fish into cubes.

Break crab into bite-size portions. Squid into small rings.

Retain the heads and shells of prawns, crabs and the fish head for stock, and place in a large saucepan, adding ginger and garlic paste and salt.

Stir and simmer over a low heat for an hour, strain stock through a fine sieve into large clean pot.

Soak Palmyra root flour in 4 cups of water for 30 minutes, and rinse until water is clear.

Dry-roast coriander seeds, cumin seeds, black peppercorns until golden and dry chillies are crisp and fragrant.

Grind the above spices in a grinder or blender, adding onions to make a smooth paste, fold in the Palmyra flour into this stock and season with salt.

Add the ground paste into seafood stock over medium heat, adding rice, fresh curry leaves and chilli powder according to your taste, and stir.

Allow to cook for a further 15 minutes or until rice is almost cooked, next add green beans, jack fruit and prepared seafood. Stir through and slow cook for 10 minutes.

Finally add spinach, season with salt, pepper, and tamarind pulp to taste.

Mulligatawny Soup

I introduced a curry-flavoured soup, Mulligatawny Soup, which originated from Tamil Nadu in Southern India. It means 'pepper water', and it was made from meat stock. I liked making a stock beforehand because that way it adds more flavour to the soup. Many customers enjoyed this soup with a crusty bread roll, it's great on a winter's night by adding vegetables into the meat it becomes a wholesome soup. In Sri Lanka we have it as a side dish and eat it with string hoppers similar to rice noodles. I made a variety of curries and one of my favourites was the Kofta Curry made from lamb mince. I always made sure I bought the best quality first grade meat; this dish can also be made with chicken, beef or pork.

Mulligatawny Soup

INGREDIENTS (STOCK)

1.5 kg chicken (with bones) OR 1 kg veal shanks
OR 1 kg beef (with bones), cut into large pieces
2 medium onions
4 cloves garlic, whole
5 cm piece of ginger, bruised
2 sprigs fresh curry leaves
2 ripe tomatoes
1 tablespoon peppercorns
1 cinnamon stick
5 litres water
Salt to taste

INGREDIENTS (SOUP)

250 g potatoes
250 g carrots
250 g celery
125 g red onions
2 tablespoons coriander seeds
1 tablespoon fennel seeds
1 teaspoon cumin seeds
1 teaspoon turmeric powder
2 tablespoons cracked black pepper
2 cups coconut milk
Juice of 1 lime
Salt

METHOD

To make stock, add water to a stockpot, along with the chopped onions, curry leaves, peppercorns, garlic, ginger, cinnamon stick, tomatoes, meat and salt to taste.

Allow stock to boil over a moderate heat, and simmer for 2 hours.

Continuously skim residue from stock during cooking time.

Strain stock into a deep bowl and set aside.

Remove meat from bones and dice into bite-size pieces and set aside.

In a shallow pan, dry-roast coriander seeds, fennel seeds, cumin seeds and cracked pepper over a low to medium heat.

Grind spices coarsely in a grinder or blender.

Peel vegetables, cut into cubes and replace stock into a large heavy base saucepan over a moderate heat.

Add grounded spices, turmeric powder, vegetables and meat to the prepared stock, and cook until tender.

Reduce heat, pour in coconut milk, stir and allow simmer for 10 minutes.

Remove from heat, adding limejuice, salt, and pepper to taste.

This soup is traditionally served with String Hoppers (rice noodles) or alternatively it can be enjoyed on its own as a hearty winter soup, served with crusty bread roll.

Sunny's Fruit Cocktail

Sunny's Fruit Cocktail

INGREDIENTS

2 cups canned pineapple juice
¼ cup apple, finely chopped
½ cup cucumber, chopped
¼ cup orange, cut into segments
2.5 cm fresh root ginger, peeled and finely chopped
Juice of ½ a lemon
½ banana
1 sprig mint leaves
Ice-cubes
Salt to taste

METHOD

Pour the pineapple juice into a blender and run on low speed, mixing in the rest of the ingredients gradually.

Increase the speed and blend for a minute.

Add ice-cubes to obtain a smooth liquid. (If it is too thick add more ice-cubes to thin it.)

Pour into flute glasses with extra ice-cubes and mint leaves.

Mixed Fruit Punch

Mixed Fruit Punch

INGREDIENTS

3 cups watermelon, seeds removed
and cut into cubes
½ teaspoon lemon juice
1 tablespoon lemon squash
1 cup orange squash
Crushed ice
1 cup cold water
Sugar to taste
½ tablespoon fresh ginger, grated
½ apple, finely chopped

METHOD

Place cubed melon in a blender and run on a low speed, adding the rest of the fruit mixers.

Add sugar, crushed ice, water and pour into tall glasses.

Decorate with chopped apple pieces.

Serve chilled with crushed ice.

Honey And Almond Drink

INGREDIENTS

2 cups full cream milk
2 cups cold water
100 g almond flakes
¼ cup pure honey
1 teaspoon rose water OR rose essence
A few saffron strands

METHOD

Soak almonds in ½ cup of hot water for one hour and grind to a fine paste.

Add the rest of water and blend to obtain a smooth liquid.

Heat milk and honey in a pan and stir until dissolved, add the saffron strands and rose essence to taste.

Add honey according to taste.

When the milk mixture is cold, add the almond mixture to milk and chill before serving.

Sri Lankan Iced Coffee

There are many ways of making iced coffee. As I remember, I always bought coffee from Island Coffee House on Galle Road. Just driving by that shop you could smell the beautiful aroma of fresh roasting coffee beans. Using the same recipe, fresh coffee powder was used. First you bring the water to the boil, add the coffee and simmer gently for 15 minutes. Let it stand and filter through a nylon sieve, or muslin cloth. But these days you can take the easy way out by either using a plunger with freshly ground coffee, or using your favourite instant coffee and follow the recipe below. It is the next best thing!

Sri Lankan Iced Coffee

INGREDIENTS

3¾ litres boiling hot water

12 dessertspoons good instant coffee or
freshly ground strong coffee (your preference)

1½ tins sweetened condensed milk

½ cup caster sugar

2 tablespoons brandy

2 teaspoons vanilla extract

½ teaspoon essence of almond

METHOD

Bring water to the boil and dissolve instant coffee
or if using fresh ground coffee use a plunger to
make coffee. Add sugar and let it cool.

Add the rest of the ingredients stir well.

Serve chilled.

Non-alcoholic drinks are very popular among Sri Lankan women at lunch or dinner parties. Many of my friends love these refreshing drinks and they are great during summer. Enjoy these easy-to-make drinks at home or for your next dinner party. Most ingredients can be bought at Sri Lankan, Indian or Asian supermarkets and most of them are not costly. Some drinks are sweet and others sour and many are consumed as a digestive beverage.

Moor (Sour Lassi)

Moor (Sour Lassi)

INGREDIENTS

4 cups natural yoghurt
8 cups cold water
1 Spanish onion, finely chopped
2 green chillies, de-seeded and
finely chopped
1 teaspoon salt
1 teaspoon dry-roasted cumin seeds

METHOD

Place the yoghurt in a blender and whip until
creamy, adding the water a little at a time.

Add salt to taste.

Pour into chilled glasses.

Sprinkle with chopped onions, green chillies and
a dash of dry roasted cumin seeds.

Mango Lassi

INGREDIENTS

4 cups creamy yoghurt
2 tablespoons castor sugar
2 cup mango pulp (Alfonso Mango
Pulp can be bought from supermarkets)
otherwise use fresh mangoes
1 cup water
1 cup crushed ice

METHOD

Place all the ingredients in a blender and whip until smooth and forms a rich texture.

Serve in chilled glasses.

NB: There are other variations: Plain Lassi or Rose Flavoured Lassi. Both are very refreshing.

Falooda

Falooda is a sweet refreshing drink hailing from India. It has the rose flavour and the sweet basil seeds that when added to the drink gives a crunchy but jelly like texture. This drink is great during summer months and is equally enjoyable at lunch and dinner parties. There are many variations, and most of the ingredients are readily available in Indian, Sri Lankan and Asian supermarkets.

Falooda

INGREDIENTS

4 cups full cream milk OR skim milk
1 tablespoon sweet basil seeds (Takmaria), soaked in ½ cup cold water
10 tablespoons rose-flavoured syrup
2 tablespoons vermicelli, soaked in 1 cup hot water
Agar, made into coloured jelly cubes
1 cup crushed ice

METHOD

Place all the ingredients in a jug and stir well.

Add crushed ice and chill before serving. (If you find it too sweet add more milk or water to dilute.)

Some serve it with a scoop of vanilla ice cream.

Bread & Rice

Roti Channai is so versatile—there are so many variations. In Sri Lanka we call it Gothamba Roti and Indians and Malaysians call it Roti Channai. These are some of the many variations: Plain Roti, Egg Roti, Kothu Roti, Roti filled with meat, fish or vegetarian spicy filling of your choice.

Gothamba Roti (Roti Channai)

Gothamba Roti (Roti Channai)

INGREDIENTS

3 cups plain flour
1¼ cups cold water
1 teaspoon salt
1 cup sunflower oil OR
coconut oil

METHOD

Sift flour into a large bowl.

Add salt and water a little at a time, kneading to make fine soft dough.

Make golf-ball-size round balls and place in a square ceramic dish.

Cover with oil, seal and set aside. (It needs to soak in the oil for 6 hours).

Place each ball on a flat surface, such as a cutting board or a stainless steel bench top.

Use your fingertips to flatten the ball, and use a rolling pin to make a large square the size of dinner plate (You can make it as thin as you like) working with your hands and finger tips.

Place each one over a low to medium heat grill and cook both sides by turning them with a pair of tongs. (These can also be cooked on a gas BBQ that has a flat grill plate or in a large frying pan).

Fold them in half and they are then ready to eat.

EGG ROTI VARIATION

Before cooking the roti, beat a few eggs.

Cook one side of the roti, turn it over pour some of the egg mixture.

When it begins to cook, fold roti in half and continue until well cooked.

KOTHU ROTI VARIATION

After rotis are cooked, chop them coarsely into strips.

Use some leftover curry any type of meat such as lamb, beef or chicken cut into cubes. Set aside.

Add a little oil into a wok and fry onions until golden, then add green chillies, shredded cabbage
and a few beaten eggs and stir to scramble.

Add prepared meat stir, and gravy from the curry, next add the coarsely chopped rotis, salt and cracked black pepper to taste.

ROTI WITH FILLING OF YOUR CHOICE

Before the rotis are cooked, use a curry you have already made, and remove meat from the gravy and dice finely.

Add sliced onions, shredded cabbage and diced boiled potato cubes and mix through adding little gravy to coat the meat.

Cook roti on both sides and place on a flat surface, then place 2 tablespoons of filling of your choice, bring the two sides together to the middle of the roti and fold into a firm tight parcel.

Cook on grill to seal.

Hoppers (Appam)

Hoppers (Appam)

INGREDIENTS

750 g rice flour
250 g plain flour
2 slices of stale bread, left over from a few
days
2 tablespoons white sugar
2 sachets dry yeast
½ cup lukewarm water
1½ cups coconut milk
1 teaspoon bicarbonate of soda
2 teaspoons salt

METHOD

Dissolve yeast in lukewarm water, stir until dissolved and set aside for half an hour to rise.

Soak bread in warm water and break it up until it softens.

Mix rice flour, salt, the soaked bread, sugar and the yeast mixture to form a soft batter.

Cover dough with cling wrap and leave overnight to rise.

Next day add enough coconut milk to the batter and stir well with a wooden spoon, making sure it coats the back of the spoon. (If the batter has not risen due to climate, add the bicarbonate of soda half an hour before cooking time.)

Heat a hopper pan with side handles, and grease it with canola oil or cooking spray. When hot pour in ½ a ladle of the batter.

Lift the pan with side handles, and give it a circular twist till the pan is coated right around with the batter.

Cover with a tight fitting lid and cook over low to medium heat until sides or border is crisp, golden brown and lacy with a soft centre.

NB: If making egg hoppers, break egg into the centre of the batter whilst cooking hoppers.
NB: To prevent the hoppers from sticking to the pan, fry the yolk of an egg in the hopper pan before preparing hoppers.

Kiri Bath

This is a simple, traditional Sinhalese dish without which no auspicious menu is complete. Even in the poorest of homes, it is a must on Sinhalese New Year's Day and it is served for breakfast on the first day of every month. This rice dish could be served with a meat dish, Miris Malu, or Katta Sambol. It is delicious with grated palm (jaggery) and bananas.

Kiri Bath

INGREDIENTS

4 cups long grain rice OR red country rice
6 cups water
4 cups coconut milk
Salt to taste

METHOD

Wash the rice, and then add water and salt.

Bring it to the boil, reduce heat and cover, and continue to cook over a low heat until the rice is soft and water is absorbed.

Stir in the coconut milk and simmer, stirring through until rice is soft and creamy.

Cool slightly and turn onto a flat dish, then even out the sides and the top with a knife.

When cold, cut Kiri Bath into diamond shapes.

Kiri bath can be served with coastal fish curry or miris malu and marci sambal.

Basic Pittu

INGREDIENTS

2 cups rice flour, roasted
1 cup scraped coconut OR 1 cup desiccated
coconut, soaked in ¼ cup warm milk
Salt to taste
2 cups extra coconut milk to moisten pittu
after cooking or to serve at table

METHOD

Place the rice flour in a food processor, using a sharp blade, gradually add enough water and salt to make granules and flakes.

Pour mixture into Pittu cylinders or micro wave safe cups alternating with coconut mixture and flour mixture until filled.

Once Pittu moulds are filled, set aside until ready to steam.

Place Pittu moulds over boiling water, cover and steam for 10-15 minutes.

Once steamed, allow to cool.

Gently remove Pittus from moulds by pushing the back of the mould with a handle of a wooden spoon.

PRAWN VARIATION

INGREDIENTS

250 g green prawns, shelled and deveined

1 large Spanish onion, finely chopped

4 hot green chillies, finely chopped

½ cup drumstick leaves OR continental parsley chopped coarsely

Salt to taste

METHOD

Chop prawn into small pieces.

Dice onions, green chillies and drumstick leaves.

Add salt to taste.

Mix all ingredients together and fold into the flour mixture.

Steam in a Pittu steamer or in an ordinary steamer.

As soon as steam starts to come out from the top cover, steam for further 5 minutes.

Remove from steamer by pushing through with the back of a wooden spoon onto a flat plate.

NB: I cook Pittu in the microwave using microwave safe moulds. First make a small layer of scraped coconut. Then add the flour mixture, repeat with coconut and cook on a high temperature for 2–3 minutes. This alternative cooking method makes perfect Pittu. Pour fresh or warmed coconut milk to moisten pittu.

Fried Fish Pittu

INGREDIENTS

250 g fish fillets, boneless
1 Spanish onion, finely chopped
4 green chillies, finely chopped
1 sprig fresh curry leaves
1 teaspoon chilli powder
Salt to taste
Sunflower oil for frying

METHOD

Cut fish into small cubes and marinate in chilli powder and season with salt.

Heat oil in a wok over a medium to hot heat and deep-fry fish until crispy and golden.

Finely chop onion, green chillies and fresh curry leaves and mix together.

Add ingredients to Pittu mixture. (Follow main Pittu recipe page 61.)

Fill the special Pittu steamer with mixture, and steam.

As soon as steam starts to come out from the top cover, steam for further 5 minutes.

Remove from steamer by pushing through with the back of a wooden spoon onto a flat plate.

Serve with a side dish of Coconut Milk. Pittu is best served with Fried Fish Curry, Prawn Curry, Mutton Curry and not forgetting Marci Sambal.

Uncle Mahendra & Aunty Pathmini

Indians call this beautiful aromatic rice and meat dish Biriyani, but in Sri Lanka we call it Buriiyani. The best Biriyani that I have ever tasted was made by Mohamed, a special Chef who came over to my late Periappa Mahendra's home. Mohamed came on special Sundays to make this dish. He would arrive early in the morning and my uncle would always be waiting anxiously to get the shopping list so he could go and buy all the fresh ingredients from the market-the onions, tomatoes, fresh coriander, hot green chillies, the special spices and the meat. I would always stand around and watch so I could learn some secrets from him. A lot of preparation went into making this dish. Mohamed would peel and slice onions so fine and grind the ginger and garlic to a thick paste. He would pan-roast the spices and then grind them, and make a thick paste out of raw cashews that he used in the curry. Some of the cashews would be used on the last layer of the rice. He also used soaked saffron strands in milk. He cooked this dish in a large heavy based vessel, as it needed space to cook this exotic dish. It involves very lengthy preparation. He would keep stirring the pot from time to time, making sure that it did not stick to the bottom of the large vessel, as it would be all in vain if it did! Endless varieties of ingredients went into the pot as cooking time progressed, but it was worth it. The aromatic smells that lingered in the air were just sensational. And the taste! I still remember the beautiful flavours of the fresh coriander, the spices and the aromatic rice. Mohamed's Moghul Biriyani is one recipe I grew up with. My Mum made it for us and I do for my children and their children. This dish can be made with lamb, beef or chicken.

Biriyani

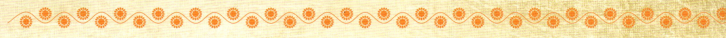

INGREDIENTS

1 kg basmati rice OR long grain (super fine) rice
8 cups water
1 kg diced lamb
1 kg white onions OR Spanish onions, thinly sliced
125 g ginger, finely ground
125 g garlic, finely ground
125 g hot green chillies
1 bunch of mint leaves, finely chopped
1 bunch of fresh coriander leaves, finely chopped
½ bunch of coriander for garnishing, finely chopped
250 g ripe tomatoes, finely chopped
250 g raw cashew nuts, ground to a fine paste
2 teaspoons turmeric powder
1 teaspoon chilli powder
2.5 cm cinnamon stick
6 cloves
6 cardamom seeds
½ cup milk
125 g ghee
1 teaspoon rose essence
500 g natural yoghurt
1 teaspoon saffron strands
1 teaspoon orange food colouring
Salt to taste

METHOD

Cut meat into 2.5 cm thick cubes.

Marinate the lamb in 250 g of yoghurt, chilli and turmeric powder and refrigerate for 3–4 hours, or overnight.

Dry-roast the cinnamon, cardamom and cloves in a frying pan until fragrant, over a low heat and grind to a fine powder.

Wash rice in water until water is clear of all starch, and place in a heavy base saucepan with 8 cups of water and cook over a high heat, reduce heat, cover with lid and cook for further 5 minutes. Leave it to cool.

Meanwhile, using a food grinder make a thick paste with the remaining yoghurt and ground cashew nuts, and then set aside.

Melt ghee in a large heavy base saucepan over a medium heat.

Add the onions and fry until golden brown.

Add the tomatoes and cook until soft and sauce is thick, then add green chillies, ground garlic, ginger and spices.

Sauté all of these ingredients until they are infused and aromatic.

Next add marinated meat and three quarters of the yoghurt and cashew paste and stir over low heat.

Add coriander and mint leaves and cook meat until soft and tender.

Stir from time to time, making sure it does not stick to the bottom of the pan and then remove from heat.

Dissolve saffron strands, orange food colouring and rose essence in warm milk.

Spread a layer of the cooked meat mixture evenly into a large deep baking dish, and then cover with a layer of cooked rice.

Continue to layer the meat and rice evenly until the dish is completely covered, making sure that the last layer is covered with rice.

Using the remaining yoghurt and cashew paste, spread evenly over the top layer of rice.

Sprinkle the saffron milk mixture and finely chopped coriander over the rice, cover with lid or foil and bake in a moderate oven for 45 minutes.

Biriyani is a very rich Mogul rice dish; it is so flavoursome that it can be eaten on its own, or accompanied with cucumber and yoghurt, Korma Curry, Raal Appam and Date Chutney.

Savoury Rice

Savoury Rice

INGREDIENTS

10 chicken drumsticks OR 1 kg thigh fillets OR

1 kg chicken breast, cut into cubes

250 g medium green prawns, de-veined

1 large Spanish onion, thinly sliced

4 cloves garlic

250 g red capsicums cut into small cubes

125 g green peas (fresh or frozen)

2 ripe tomatoes, finely chopped

4 cups short grain rice

1 tin tomato puree (400 ml)

½ teaspoon Spanish saffron

1 cup black and green olives

8–10 cups chicken stock

½ cup olive oil

Salt to taste

METHOD

Heat olive oil in a heavy base saucepan.

Pan-fry chicken on all sides until golden brown.

Simmer until half-cooked.

Add sliced onion, chopped garlic, tomato, tomato purée and add salt to taste. Cook a further 10 minutes.

Add rice and cook until most of the oil is absorbed.

Bring the stock to the boil in another saucepan and mix in the saffron and salt to taste.

Add the diced capsicum, olives and green peas into the rice mixture folding until well blended.

Now transfer rice and chicken mixture into an ovenproof dish.

Pour the boiling hot stock mixture over the rice and chicken mixture, then add green prawns and cook in a fairly low oven for 1 hour.

Mutton Pillau

Mutton Pillau

INGREDIENTS (STOCK)
500 g mutton off the bone
1 large Spanish onion OR white onion, thinly sliced
6 cloves garlic
2.5 cm piece green ginger
4 hot green chillies (use less if you want a milder flavour)
2 teaspoons coriander seeds
10 cups water
4 beef stock cubes
Salt to taste

INGREDIENTS (RICE)
4 cups basmati rice
4 cloves garlic, ground to a fine paste
2.5 cm piece ginger ground
2 teaspoons cumin seeds
4 cardamom pods, bruised
4 cloves
2.5 cm stick cinnamon
4 tablespoons ghee
1 cup natural yoghurt
8 cups beef stock

INGREDIENTS FOR GARNISHING
1 large white onion, sliced into rings
2 tablespoons ghee
4 hard-boiled eggs, sliced

NB: If mutton (goat) is not available lean lamb can be substituted.

METHOD FOR STOCK

Cut mutton into large cubes and set aside.

In a grinder, add garlic, ginger and green chillies and grind to a fine paste. Set aside.

In a mortar and pestle, bruise coriander seeds to release flavour.

In a heavy base saucepan, add meat, water, ground paste, bruised coriander and salt to taste.

Simmer over a medium heat until meat is almost tender. Remove from heat.

Drain and retain meat in a bowl and pour remaining stock into a 2 litre jug (dilute with stock cubes and water to make up 8 cups of stock). Set aside.

METHOD FOR RICE

Wash and drain rice.

Heat ghee in a deep heavy base saucepan and fry onions until golden over a medium heat.

Add garlic, ginger paste, cumin seeds, cloves, cinnamon stick, bruised cardamom pods and sauté until fragrant.

Add mutton and mix through well until meat is well coated.

Allow the meat to brown.

While meat is browning, boil reserved stock over a medium heat.

While stock is re-heating, add drained rice to meat mixture and stir and reduce heat to low.

Fold yoghurt into rice and meat until well coated.

Gradually pour the boiling stock into the rice and meat mixture and mix through.

Cover and cook rice for 15–20 minutes.

When rice is cooked, fluff with a fork.

When ready to serve, garnish with fried onion rings and slices of hard- boiled eggs.

METHOD FOR GARNISHING

In a frying pan, heat ghee over a medium heat and fry onion rings until golden and crispy. Drain on absorbent paper.

Now slice hard-boiled eggs thinly. Garnish the dish using the fried onion rings and sliced eggs.

Vegetable Pillau

Vegetable Pillau

INGREDIENTS (RICE)

1 kg basmati rice
8 cups vegetable stock
2 tablespoons ghee
2 teaspoons salt
2 large potatoes, peeled and cut into cubes
3 medium carrots, peeled and cut into cubes
¼ cauliflower, cut into florets
250 g green peas (fresh OR frozen)
2 green capsicums, cut into cubes
1 large white onion, finely diced
2 ripe tomatoes, finely chopped
½ bunch fresh coriander leaves, finely chopped
¼ cup water
Salt to taste

INGREDIENTS (PILLAU PASTE)

2 medium white onions OR Spanish onions, finely sliced
6 cloves garlic, finely ground
2.5 cm piece fresh ginger, finely ground
4 green chillies, finely chopped
3 cardamom pods
3 cloves
3 teaspoons white poppy seeds
1 cinnamon stick
1 teaspoon chilli powder
1 teaspoon turmeric powder

INGREDIENTS FOR GARNISHING

1 teaspoon saffron powder, dissolved in water
1 tablespoon water
125 g cashew nuts
125 g raisins
2 white onions, thinly sliced

METHOD

Combine onion, ginger, garlic and white poppy seeds in a spice grinder or mortar and grind or pound with a pestle to form a smooth paste.

Add green chillies, turmeric and chilli powder and blend until finely ground. Set aside while preparing the rest of ingredients.

Dry-fry the cinnamon, cardamom and cloves until light and fragrant, and grind to a fine powder. Set aside

Heat ghee in heavy bottom saucepan over medium heat add thinly sliced onions and fry until golden brown.

Add tomato and cook over medium heat, stirring occasionally for 5 minutes or until tomato is soft. Add salt and ground pillau paste and stir through until well mixed. Next add cubed carrots and potatoes into masala, when this is half cooked, mix in the cauliflower, capsicums and green peas.

Finally add the chopped coriander leaves and set aside as you prepare the rice.

Wash rice and allow it to drain thoroughly in a colander.

Boil stock in a separate pan.

In another heavy base saucepan heat 3 tablespoons of ghee, then add drained rice and fry until sealed.

Pour boiling stock over the rice whilst adding salt to taste.

Cook rice on a low heat for approximately 12 minutes or until cooked.

In a frying pan melt 2 tablespoons of ghee and fry onion until golden then set aside.

In a separate pan, toss cashew nuts over medium heat until golden adding raisins until they change colour.

Arrange a layer of rice and a layer of the vegetable mixture in alternative layers ending with a rice layer on top.

Sprinkle the rice with saffron mixture generously and bake in a slow oven for 20 minutes.

Garnish rice with fried onion slices, roasted cashew nuts and raisins.

This rice dish works best with Mutton Poriyal, Prawn Curry, Tomato and Onion Sambal or Brinjal Pahi.

Yellow Rice

Yellow Rice

INGREDIENTS

5 cups long grain rice OR basmati rice
4 cups thick coconut milk
4 cups boiling water
3 teaspoons turmeric
3 cubes chicken stock
1 large sprig fresh curry leaves
2 teaspoons salt

INGREDIENTS FOR GARNISHING

2 eggs, lightly beaten
1 large white onion, thinly sliced
¼ cup sultanas
Sunflower oil for frying

METHOD

Wash and drain rice thoroughly in a colander.

In a separate saucepan bring coconut milk, water, turmeric, chicken stock cubes, fresh curry leaves and salt to the boil.

Gently pour this stock into the rice.

Then reduce heat, cover with a lid and simmer for 20 minutes.

Remove fresh curry leaves.

METHOD FOR GARNISHING

Using a non-stick saucepan, make thin omelettes with the beaten eggs.

Place 2 or 3 on top of each other, then roll tightly and cut into strips.

Pan-fry onions until golden and set aside.

In the same frying pan, toss sultanas until they change colour.

Arrange the cooked rice on a serving platter, cover with shredded eggs and sprinkle with fried onion slices and sultanas.

NB: Dilute tins of coconut milk to make up thin milk as you do not want the rice to be too rich in flavour. Golden Yellow Rice is a beautiful fragrant rice dish and can be eaten with Chicken Poriyal, Pork Sorpotel, Tomato and Onion Sambal or Roll Cutlets.

Accompaniments

Dhal Rasam

Dhal Rasam

INGREDIENTS

1 cup red lentils
2 dried chillies
1 clove garlic, finely chopped
1 teaspoon turmeric powder
2 teaspoons coriander seeds
1 teaspoon cumin seeds
1 teaspoon black peppercorns
½ teaspoon tamarind fruit, soaked in
¼ cup of water or 2 tablespoons pulp
2 ripe tomatoes, finely chopped
8 cups water
Salt to taste

INGREDIENTS FOR GARNISHING

2 large onions, finely chopped
1 sprig fresh curry leaves
2 dried chillies, finely sliced
1 teaspoon mustard seeds
1 tablespoon Sunflower oil

METHOD

Wash lentils and soak in cold water for one hour.

Meanwhile, dry-roast the coriander, cumin and pepper in a heavy base pan over a medium heat until golden and fragrant.

Cool, then grind to a fine powder in a blender and set aside.

Place the soaked dhal with four cups of water in a heavy base saucepan, adding the garlic, tomatoes, turmeric powder and simmer over a low heat.

Allow to cook, continuously stirring until the lentils are soft forming a thick consistency.

In a separate saucepan, add 4 cups of water and bring to the boil.

Reduce heat and whilst pouring the water into the pureed dhal, add the ground spice mixture, tamarind pulp and salt to taste.

Gently stir and reduce heat to low and simmer for a further five minutes.

In a separate frying pan add oil and toss mustard seeds until it crackles, next fry finely chopped onions until golden, dried chillies, and fresh curry leaves and stir until aromatic.

Add this to the Dhal Rasam and serve hot.

Rasam is mainly served with vegetarian curry dishes. It can also be served as a spicy soup with crusty bread on the side.

Tomato Rasam

INGREDIENTS

500 g ripe tomatoes
2 onions, finely chopped
2 cloves garlic, finely chopped
2 green chillies, finely chopped
1 sprig curry leaves
1 teaspoon turmeric
6 cups water
Salt to taste

INGREDIENTS (RASAM)

2 teaspoons coriander seeds
1½ tablespoons cumin seeds
½ teaspoon black peppercorns
2 dried chillies

INGREDIENTS FOR GARNISHING

1 medium-size white onion,
finely chopped
1 sprig fresh curry leaves
1 teaspoon black mustard seeds
2 tablespoons Sunflower oil

METHOD

Wash the tomatoes and cut into large cubes.

Then place in a large saucepan with 6 cups of water, bring to the boil and simmer until soft.

Strain the stock with a fine sieve into a saucepan, discard tomato and set aside. (The soup has got to be clear for the preparation of rasam.)

Add salt to taste.

Dry-roast the coriander, cumin and peppercorn seeds in a heavy base frying pan. Make sure you evenly roast all ingredients until fragrant.

Next add the dried chillies and toss until they puff up. Set aside.

Place these ingredients in a grinder or mortar and pestle and grind to make a coarse powder, and then set aside.

Place the tomato stock on a medium heat and bring to the boil.

Add the ground spice mixture and cook on high heat and bring the tomato stock to the boil. Reduce heat.

In a frying pan, add oil add mustard seeds and fry until it crackles, next add onions until golden, curry leaves and stir until aromatic, add this to the tomato rasam.

Rasam (Pepper Water)

INGREDIENTS

3 tablespoons coriander seeds
1 teaspoon cumin seeds
1 whole garlic pod
1 teaspoon black peppercorns
2 dried red chillies torn
1 sprig fresh curry leaves
1 teaspoon tamarind paste
4 cups water
Salt to taste

METHOD

Place coriander, cumin, garlic and peppercorns in a mortar and pestle, and pound or in a spice grinder and grind coarsely, then set aside.

Then place tamarind, water, ground spices, and crushed garlic, curry leaves and chilli into a medium-size saucepan and cook over a high heat for 10 minutes and bring to the boil.

Reduce heat to low and simmer for 5 minutes.

Add salt to taste and remove from heat.

Spices, Mixtures & Curry Pastes

Spices, Mixtures And Curry Pastes

The word 'curry' originated from the Tamil word 'kari', which refers to any food that is cooked in a curry sauce. Curry powders come in many different blends. These powders are available for one's convenience, bringing beautiful exotic flavours to your dinner table. When I was growing up, I remember the dry ingredients were bought from spice merchants and stored in a meat safe. The basic curry powders were always prepared well ahead and stored in a large tin in a cool place, and made at home using the best ingredients, fine spices, fresh curry leaves, lemongrass, and rampé. On a daily basis, the Appu and Sinna Appu were on hand to assist, and therefore according the menu of the day, the spices were dry-roasted or grounded raw on the grinding stone. They were mainly the chilli, coriander, cumin, fennel, and turmeric. For some reason by grinding these ingredients, it gave body and texture to the curry that was been prepared on that day.

It still feels like it was only yesterday when the Appu, Kandiah got Ponnambalam, a very well spoken English scholar to come and work for my grandparents. I will never know why he ended up working there when he spoke so well, but I never really got a chance to ask him because I was only a child myself! Kandiah made him grind all these different spices into round balls and place them on a silver plated round platter. To preserve them he added clumps of rock salt on it so that whatever was left over could be used the next day.

Curry Powder For Dry Curries (Seafood And Meat)

INGREDIENTS

500 g fennel seeds
100 g cumin seeds
150 g coriander seeds
50 g black peppercorns
50 g cardamom pods
50 g cinnamon sticks
30 g fenugreek seeds
100 g cloves
100 g red dry chillies
15 sprigs fresh curry leaves
2.5cm rampé (pandan leaf),
cut into small pieces

METHOD

Mix all the spices together.

Use a heavy base pan or wok and dry-roast the spices, tossing them frequently so they do not burn. Cook the spices until they give a rich spicy aroma. (These spices can be dry-roasted separately on a slow fire, continuously stirring and turning so they roast evenly to a golden brown colour.)

Pick up a few seeds with your fingertips and crush them. If they crumble they are ready. (You will know by the delightful aromatic flavour of the different spices that fills the air!)

Remove from heat and cool.

Use a food processor, blender or grinder to grind the powder.

Store in an airtight container. Keep in a cool place.

This special curry powder is used for Chicken Poriyal, Mutton Poriyal, Jaffna Style Crab Curry, Omelette Curry and Fried Fish Curry.

Garam Masala

INGREDIENTS

100 g coriander seeds
50 g cumin seeds
50 g cardamom pods
50 g cloves
2.5 cm cinnamon sticks
25 g black peppercorns

METHOD

Mix all the ingredients together and dry-roast in a wok or frying pan until golden brown in colour.

Place roasted spices in a grinder or blender and grind to a fine powder.

Store in an airtight container in a cool place.

Jaffna Curry Powder

INGREDIENTS

500 g dried chillies
2 teaspoons turmeric powder
200 g fennel seeds
500 g coriander seeds
50 g fenugreek seeds
100 g pepper corns
8 sprigs fresh curry leaves

METHOD

Remove the stems and seeds and snap each chilli into 2–3 pieces, then set aside.

Dry-roast individual spices or add all the spices together in a heavy base pan tossing them frequently until they give a rich and spicy fragrance.

Add the dried chillies over a medium heat until they soften and puff up, making sure that they do not burn.

Pick up a seed and crush it with your fingers, if it crumbles, then it is ready for grinding. Allow to cool.

Place mixture into a dry food processor, and grind mixture to a fine powder. Mix in turmeric powder.

Store in an airtight container. Keep in a cool place.

This Curry Powder can be used for various curries with chicken, fish, lamb, mutton and pork. For a basic curry recipe, add these spices, add coconut milk to blend with tamarind or lime juice to taste. It creates a traditional Jaffna style curry.

Special Roasted Curry Powder

INGREDIENTS

500 g fennel seeds
100 g cumin seeds
150 g coriander seeds
100 g red dried chillies
50 black peppercorns
50 g cardamom pods
50 g cinnamon sticks
100 g cloves
15 sprigs fresh curry leaves
2.5 cm rampé (pandan leaf)
pieces, finely sliced

METHOD

Use a heavy base frying pan to dry-roast the spices.

Heat pan and add spices, cooking them over a medium heat and tossing them frequently until they are rich in flavour and aromatic.

Add the fresh curry leaves and rampé and cook over medium heat to release their flavour into the spice mix, shaking and tossing the pan so the ingredients are evenly roasted to a golden brown colour.

Pick up a few seeds into your fingertips and crush them; if they crumble they are ready. (You will know by the delightful aromatic flavours that will linger in the air.) Allow to cool.

Grind the spices by using a food processor or blender.

Store in an airtight container and keep in a cool place.

This curry powder is mainly used for Crab Curry, Chicken Poriyal, Mutton Poriyal, Brinjal and Dry Fish Curry, Omelette Curry and Prawn Thiyal.

Aunty Rajes Jeganathan was a big part of my life. I lived with her and her family for a while before I migrated to Australia. She was closely related to my Mum and had a large family. Adjoining her home, she had an annexe that she had let out to me when I had just given birth to my first child, Sunny. Aunty Rajes was such a loving, caring and giving person and loved me as if I was her own child. She would tell me as a rule that if a mother is feeding her baby, she should not eat spicy food but should have other spices that fasten healing, and that is how I came to know about the 'Sarakku Curries'. She told me that these curries were old ancient recipes made to help heal the body, and were extremely good for me.

She had a maid called Kottu Ayah, which means 'skinny', who I absolutely adored. She had worked at Aunty Rajes' home for years, taking care of her children and at that time there were five of them at home. Kottu Ayah had been in the family for over 30 years. I remember her when I was a child. She was kind and held a special place in my heart. As it was quite a big household, Kottu Ayah only helped in the kitchen at special times when asked. I remember Aunty Rajes asking her to prepare this curry for me on this day. Aunty Rajes was giving her all the instructions about how the spices had to be prepared to make this curry. On this day, she made the King Fish version, which was delightful. I would thereafter, often ask her to prepare this special curry for me. This particular curry was made with coriander, cumin, black pepper and fresh curry leaves with roasted ground coconut. All these spices are known for their goodness and health benefits such as improved digestion and intestinal health.

Sarakku Thull Curry Powder

INGREDIENTS

500 g coriander seeds
4 sprigs fresh curry leaves
10 g turmeric powder
400 g cumin seeds
25 g black peppercorns

METHOD

Heat a heavy base pan to a medium heat.

Add coriander seeds and dry-roast until they develop a sweet flavour, making sure you constantly shake the pan; do not burn the seeds. They have to be light golden in colour.

Remove from heat and place in a separate bowl.

Dry-roast the cumin seeds until they form a nutty flavour. Set aside.

While you dry-fry the black peppercorns, add fresh sprigs of curry leaves and stir over medium heat until crispy. Remove from heat.

Cool before grinding the spices in a food processor or spice grinder until it forms a fine powder.

Mix the turmeric powder to blend well with the rest of the spices mixture.

Store in an airtight container and leave in a cool place.

This curry powder is mainly used for Fish and Chicken Sarakku Curry.

Chilli Mayonnaise

INGREDIENTS

4 whole eggs
4 teaspoons vinegar
2 cups olive oil OR salad oil
1 teaspoon salt

INGREDIENTS (CHILLI SAUCE)

6 fresh red chillies, de-seeded and
finely chopped
¼ cup caster sugar
2 cloves of garlic, thinly sliced
2 teaspoons dark soy sauce
½ cup water
1 tablespoon vegetable oil
Salt to taste

METHOD FOR MAYONNAISE

Break eggs into a bowl and whisk with an electric beater until thick.

Gently begin to pour in the oil, drop by drop, whisking constantly.

Add the vinegar and salt to taste.

As the mixture begins to thicken, increase the speed on the beater and beat until the mixture is thickened and the oil is well blended. Set aside.

METHOD FOR CHILLI SAUCE

Heat oil in a pan. Add garlic and chilli and stir-fry over medium heat for 1–2 minutes.

Add sugar and water and simmer until fairly thick.

Add soy and salt to taste and cool.

Blend to a smooth paste.

Fold into mayonnaise.

Pickles, Sambals & Chutneys

Mixed Vegetable Pickle

Mixed Vegetable Pickle

- **INGREDIENTS**

250 g red onions OR scallions, peeled and left whole
125 g carrots, peeled and cut into 2 cm long pieces
125 g green chillies, whole
125 g banana capsicums, de-seeded and cut into four quarters
125 g green beans, strings removed and cut into 2 cm strips
1 small young papaya, peeled, seeds removed and cut into bite-size pieces
250 g cucumbers, peeled, seeds removed and cut same way as papaya
2 tablespoons black mustard seeds
1 teaspoon black peppercorns
1 teaspoon turmeric powder
1 teaspoon chilli powder
2.5 cm piece young fresh root ginger, peeled and thinly chopped
1 cup white vinegar
125 g white sugar
1 cup water
Salt to taste

- **METHOD**

Use a liquidiser or good grinder to make a fine paste with the mustard seeds, black peppercorns, ginger, and chilli powder by adding a little water.

Place the water, vinegar and sugar in a medium heavy base saucepan and over a medium heat, add the ground turmeric powder, the ground chilli, ginger, mustard paste and cook until the sauce is fairly thick.

Add salt to taste and simmer gently for 10 minutes.

Place the prepared vegetables in a glass bowl and mix.

Pour in the marinade and mix well.

Store in airtight glass bottles for two days before use.

- This Mixed Vegetable Pickle can be kept for months if stored in a cool place, or in the refrigerator.

Eggplant And Yoghurt Salad

Eggplant And Yoghurt Salad

INGREDIENTS

750 g eggplant (approximately 6 medium eggplants)
1 large white onion, finely chopped
1 teaspoon ginger, grated
4 hot green chillies, de-seeded and finely cut
1 cup natural yoghurt
2 tablespoons freshly squeezed lime juice
Salt to taste

METHOD

Pre-heat the oven to 425°C.

Spray eggplants with olive oil and wrap each eggplant in foil.

Bake in a moderately hot oven for 1 hour. Remove from oven and allow eggplants to cool.

Scoop the flesh of the eggplant into a mixing bowl and coarsely mash and set aside.

Prepare all other ingredients as specified above.

Combine onions, ginger and chillies in a large mixing bowl.

In a separate bowl, whisk the yoghurt until creamy, while adding lime juice.

This salad compliments leavened breads, and vegetarian and lamb curries.

Add eggplant, yoghurt and salt to the salad.

Fold through gently until all ingredients are combined.

Crispy Fried Fish And Onion Sambal

Crispy Fried Fish And Onion Sambal

INGREDIENTS

250 g Spanish Mackerel fillets OR any
boneless fish fillet
2 large firm tomatoes, finely chopped
2 large Spanish onions, finely sliced
4 green chillies, finely chopped
Juice of 1 lime
Salt and black cracked pepper to taste
Sunflower oil for frying
INGREDIENTS (MARINADE)
1 teaspoon chilli powder
½ teaspoon turmeric
½ teaspoon salt

METHOD

Pat dry fish and cut into bite-size portions.

In a bowl, combine chilli powder, turmeric and salt.

Add bite-size fish portions and marinate for 30 minutes.

Place oil in a frying pan over a medium heat and fry fish
pieces until golden and crispy. Allow to drain on absorbent paper and set aside.

In a mixing bowl, combine onions, chillies and tomatoes.

Add salt and pepper to taste.

Add fried fish, lime juice and mix through.

Serve with rice dishes, prawn or vegetable curries.

Dry Fish And Onion Sambal

Dry Fish And Onion Sambal

INGREDIENTS

250 g salted dry King Fish OR Tuna Fish
4 green chillies, de-seeded and sliced
3 hot dried chillies, broken into pieces
2 large white onions, finely sliced
Juice of 1 lime
Salt to taste
Sunflower oil for frying
1 tablespoon olive oil

METHOD

Cut dry fish into 2.5 cm pieces and fry until crispy.

Allow to drain on absorbent paper.

In a shallow frying pan, heat olive oil over a medium heat, fry dried chillies until crisp and set aside.

In a bowl, combine the sliced onions, green chillies, and fried dried chillies and allow to cool.

Before serving, add dry fish pieces to sambal and toss.

Season with salt and lime juice.

Tomato Sambal

Tomato Sambal

INGREDIENTS

2 large tomatoes, de-seeded and finely chopped
½ cup white or red onions, finely chopped
4 red chillies, de-seeded and finely chopped
2 heaped tablespoons coriander leaves, coarsely chopped
1 green capsicum, diced into small pieces
2 tablespoons lemon juice OR lime juice, freshly squeezed
¼ cup coconut milk
Rock salt and cracked pepper to taste

METHOD

Combine onions, chillies, coriander, capsicum and tomato into a bowl and toss.

Add rock salt and cracked pepper to the sambal, according to taste.

Add freshly squeezed lemon or lime juice.

Pour the coconut milk into the sambal and gently fold through.

Refrigerate until ready to serve

This Sambal complements Biriyani, Pillau, lamb, beef and poultry curry dishes.

Seeni Sambal

INGREDIENTS

12 Spanish onions OR white onions,
finely chopped
8 tablespoons Sunflower oil
12 cloves garlic, finely chopped
2 teaspoons ginger, finely chopped
8 cardamom pods, crushed
4 teaspoons cinnamon powder
2 sprigs fresh curry leaves
8 tablespoons sugar
¼ cup tamarind juice
Juice of 1 lemon
Salt to taste

METHOD

Heat oil in a wok and fry onions, garlic and ginger until golden brown, and almost crisp.

Add all the remaining ingredients except the lemon juice and sugar.

Cook on low heat for 30–45 minutes, stirring constantly until the mixture turns dark and leaves the sides of the wok.

Add the sugar and lemon juice and stir well.

Cook for further 10 minutes and remove from heat.

Crab Sambal

INGREDIENTS

4–5 blue swimmer crabs (whole)
3 litres water
2 medium Spanish onions, finely chopped
2.5 cm piece fresh ginger, finely grated
4 green chillies, de-seeded and finely chopped
1 cup coconut milk (thick)
Lime juice and salt to taste

METHOD

Bring water to the boil in a large saucepan.

Add crabs and cook until they change colour. Drain water, and allow to cool.

Once cooled, remove flesh from the crabs and the flake meat.

Place into a separate bowl and refrigerate while preparing the rest of the ingredients.

In a mixing bowl, add onions, chillies, ginger and salt, and toss.

Add chilled crabmeat to the sambal.

Gently fold in the coconut milk.

Season with lime juice add salt according to taste.

Ginger Pachadi

Another side dish is the freshly grated young Ginger Pachadi with fresh coconut and a pinch of green chillies and red onions. There were many other side Pachadis and salads, such as freshly grated carrot that we always had at lunchtime. It was served with red onions, green chillies and cracked pepper with grated coconut and has a citrus flavour. These side dishes have been in Hindu families and in the Northern Sri Lankan region for generations. They are prepared to celebrate a happy occasion or an alms giving and families come together, each bringing a few to share.

Ginger Pachadi

INGREDIENTS

1 cup young ginger, grated
½ cup grated fresh coconut OR desiccated
coconut soaked in a ¼ cup of warm water
1 medium Spanish onion OR white onion, finely
chopped
4 green chillies, de-seeded and finely chopped
1 sprig fresh curry leaves
1 teaspoon black mustard seeds
10 black peppercorns, coarsely ground
Lemon juice OR lime juice to taste
Salt to taste
1 tablespoon Sunflower oil

METHOD

Combine grated ginger, coconut, chopped onions
and green chillies in a bowl and set aside.

Heat olive oil in a frying pan over a medium heat and
fry mustard seeds until they crackle.

Add fresh curry leaves and ground black peppercorns and sauté for 2 minutes, then allow to cool.

Next add grated ginger, onion and coconut mixture
and toss.

Season with salt and lemon juice according to taste.

CARROT VARIATION

Use the same ingredients as the Ginger Pachadi but
use 1 cup grated carrot instead of 1 cup ginger.

Marci Sambal ~ Katta Sambal

Marci Sambal ~ Katta Sambal

- **INGREDIENTS**
  10 dried red chillies
  125 g Maldives fish, coarsely ground
  1 Spanish onion OR white onion, finely chopped
  6 green chillies, chopped
  Juice of 1 lime
  Salt to taste

- **METHOD**
  Grind red chillies to a fine paste in a grinder or mortar and pestle.

  Add Maldive fish and lime juice and grind until blended.

  Gradually add green chillies and onions and continue to grind until it forms a coarse texture.

  Season with salt according to taste.

This sambal complements Pittu, Gothamba and Pol Roti, Hoppers or Kiri Bath (Milk Rice).

Many who do not know much about curry leaves (Karapincha) ask me, "Do you use this as a main ingredient to make a curry?" My answer is always "no" but it still is a very essential ingredient especially when it is used fresh because it brings out the flavours in a curry. The full flavour is released when the leaves are bruised. The leaves can be either torn or used whole. Fresh curry leaves can be bought from grocers and will keep well, provided they are wrapped. I wrap mine in newspaper. Dried leaves are sold in many Indian and Sri Lankan grocery stores, but I find that they have lost their flavour when they have been dried. All these herbs are useful for health conditions such as some digestive disorders, and they provide various other health benefits.

Karapincha And Coriander Pachadi

Karapincha And Coriander Pachadi

INGREDIENTS

1 cup fresh curry leaves (available in
supermarkets and, Indian and
Sri Lankan spice shops)
1 cup coriander leaves
1 large white onion OR Spanish onion,
finely chopped
6 green chillies
2.5 cm ginger, grated
1 clove garlic, finely chopped
1 teaspoon black peppercorns
¼ cup fresh grated coconut OR
desiccated coconut
Juice of 1 lime
Salt to taste

METHOD

Grind onions and green chillies to a coarse paste in a
grinder or food processor.

Add freshly grated coconut or desiccated coconut,
curry leaves, coriander leaves, peppercorns, garlic,
ginger and lime juice.

Continue to grind until it forms a smooth paste.

Season with salt.

This dish complements many rice dishes such as Mutton Pillau, Biriyani, Yellow Rice and all curry dishes.

I love using coriander leaves in my soups, curries, Biriyani and chutneys and as a garnish. I use the roots too because chopping them up finely really adds to the flavour. The beauty of the leaf is lost if you chop the leaves too finely, so always add the leaves at the end of the cooking time otherwise the leaves will be limp and too over-powering. Fresh coriander will only last for a couple of days. Wrap it up in newspaper or let it stand in a jug of cold water covered with cling wrap.

Coriander And Mint Chutney

Coriander And Mint Chutney

INGREDIENTS

1 cup mint leaves, washed and dried
1 cup coriander leaves, washed and dried
1 large white onion OR Spanish onion, finely chopped
2 cloves garlic
2.5 cm piece ginger
6 green chillies
4 tablespoon fresh grated coconut OR desiccated coconut
Juice of 1 lime
¼ cup water
Salt to taste

METHOD

Using a grinder or a blender, grind green chillies and onions to form a coarse paste.

Add garlic, ginger, coriander and mint leaves and continue to grind.

Gradually add coconut with water to form a smooth paste.

Add lime juice and salt to taste and blend until all ingredients are well blended and chutney in a smooth consistency.

This chutney complements Vadais, Bonda and rice dishes and can also be served as a dip with Pappadams and flat breads.

Date Chutney

I have created many of my own side dishes, chutneys and pickles because I am very passionate about experimenting with new tastes. I cook with a sense of invention and innovation and I like to try out things until I get it 'just right'. I love herbs such as coriander and mint, so I have had a go at many side dishes.

Date Chutney

INGREDIENTS

125 g seedless dates, finely chopped
125 g caster sugar
1 clove garlic, ground
2½ teaspoons chilli powder
½ teaspoon clove powder
½ teaspoon cinnamon powder
½ teaspoon black mustard seeds,
ground to a paste
125 g raisins
6 tablespoons vinegar
Salt to taste

METHOD

Place sugar and vinegar in a large saucepan over medium heat and stir until sugar has dissolved.

Add dates, chilli powder, garlic, clove powder, cinnamon powder and mustard.

Continue to cook, adding salt to taste and stirring occasionally.

Finally add raisins and stir. Reduce heat to low and simmer for 30–35 minutes, stirring occasionally until liquid has evaporated and the chutney looks smooth and glossy.

Allow to cool, then place chutney in sterilised jars and refrigerate.

This chutney is best served with rotis, rice and curry dishes. The chutney will store for many months.

Green Coconut Chutney

Green Coconut Chutney

INGREDIENTS

2 cups fresh grated coconut OR desiccated coconut
1 large white onion, chopped finely
2 cm piece fresh green ginger
10–12 green chillies, chopped
1 sprig fresh curry leaves
1 tablespoon lime juice OR lemon juice
1¼ teaspoons salt to taste

METHOD

In a grinder add onion and grind until coarse.

Add green chillies, ginger and curry leaves and continue to grind until it forms a smooth paste.

Gradually add the grated coconut with lime juice to make thick glossy chutney.

Add salt to taste.

RED CHILLI VARIATION

You can substitute fresh red chillies for the green chillies to make red chutney.

This side dish is a great accompaniment to Dosai, Chapati, Samosa, Vaddais and South East Asian leavened breads and vegetarian curries.

Pudina Chutney (Mint Chutney)

INGREDIENTS

1 cup grated fresh coconut OR
desiccated coconut
1½ cups mint leaves
1 medium onion, finely diced
2.5 cm piece fresh ginger, finely
chopped
6–8 green chillies, finely chopped
Juice of 1 lime
1 teaspoon sugar
Salt to taste

METHOD

In a grinder or food processor, place onions and green chillies, and grind to a coarse paste.

Pause for a minute and add mint leaves and grated ginger to the onion and chilli paste and continue to grind until all ingredients are well blended.

Gradually add the coconut and blend until smooth.

Add salt and sugar and lemon juice to taste and stir through the coconut mixture.

Accompany this chutney with Bondas, Ulundu Vadai, Masala Vadai, Biriyani, curry dishes or use as a dip with Pappadams.

Egg Dishes & Vegetable Curries

Aunty Naheswari

Before I migrated to Australia I lived briefly with my Aunty Naheswari, or Aunty Nahes, as we called her. She would cook her Turmeric Crusted Egg Curry in chilli with coconut milk and a hint of her special curry powder. Aunty Nahes had a daily helper, Caroline, who would get all the ingredients ready for Aunty to cook. One steamy Jaffna day, I overheard Aunty giving what at first struck me as very fussy instructions to Caroline about how the eggs for this dish had to be prepared. My aunt was always very particular about the ingredients she used. In this recipe I talk about pricking the boiled egg with a fork and then rolling it in the turmeric. All those years ago, I had heard Aunty telling Caroline "I want you to strip the leaves from the thick part of the stem of the curry leaf and prick the eggs with the stem." I heard Caroline say "why?" and Aunty Nahes told her that the full flavour of the curry leaf would only be released into the eggs if she followed this method. The instructions did not end there! While Caroline was working at it, Aunty continued giving her more instructions–how to shell the eggs, how to heat the oil and how to fry the eggs, and so on. I could sense Caroline's patience wearing thin. Aunty's every instruction was prefaced by the word "hondata", which in Singhalese loosely translates to 'means well' or 'properly'. My aunt spoke atrocious Singhalese and her accent was hilarious which reduced me to fits of laughter. The high point of this conversation came when Aunty instructed Caroline to fry the pricked egg "hondata" until it "becomes likes a pappadam." Caroline was finally at the end of her tether and said to Aunty, "if you want a pappadam, why don't you eat a pappadam? Why do you want to fry an egg until it becomes like a pappadam?" I was on the floor with laughter... But Aunty was right! The aromatic flavour really does get into the egg so much better with her technique, as the curry leaves and the stem have such a warm fragrance.

Turmeric Crusted Egg Curry

Turmeric Crusted Egg Curry

INGREDIENTS

8 hard-boiled eggs
1 teaspoon turmeric
3 medium white onions, finely chopped
3 green chillies, finely chopped
1 teaspoon dark roasted curry powder
Juice of ½ a lemon
Sunflower oil for frying
4 flakes garlic, finely sliced
4 sprigs fresh curry leaves
1 stem lemongrass thinly cut
1 teaspoon fenugreek seeds
2 tablespoons chilli powder
250 g ripe tomatoes, finely chopped
2 cups thick coconut milk
1 cup water
Salt to taste

METHOD FOR EGGS

Shell the eggs, prick them all over with a fork and rub in salt and turmeric powder.

Heat oil in a pan and shallow-fry the eggs until golden brown.

Remove from oil and drain on absorbent paper.

METHOD FOR GRAVY

Heat oil in a heavy based saucepan and fry the thinly chopped onions until golden.

Add the garlic and chopped tomatoes, and cook until soft.

Add fresh curry leaves and fenugreek seeds and stir for 1 minute.

Add chilli and turmeric powders and cook for 3 minutes.

Add coconut milk and simmer, while adding fried eggs and salt to taste.

Sprinkle Curry Powder and Cook until the gravy is thick (about 5 minutes).

Remove from heat and add lime juice to taste.

Serve with Savoury Rice, Roti Channai, Hoppers, Sambals or Beef Badun.

Omelette Curry

Omelette Curry

INGREDIENTS

8 eggs
Salt and pepper to taste
2 large white onions, finely chopped
6 green chillies, finely sliced
1 stem lemongrass, finely sliced
2 sprigs fresh curry leaves
6 dried chillies, cut into small pieces
1 tablespoon tamarind pulp
1 teaspoon fenugreek seeds
2 tablespoons chilli powder
1 teaspoon turmeric powder
2 tablespoons special dark roasted curry powder
2 cups thick coconut milk
2 cups water
Sunflower oil for frying

METHOD FOR OMELETTES

Beat eggs gently, adding salt and pepper to taste.

Use an omelette pan 20 cm in diameter.

Put in one tablespoon of oil and when hot, ladle in one quarter of the mixture and gently brown both sides cooking for about 3 minutes.

Drain on absorbent paper.

Continue to cook the rest of the egg mixture and cut them into wedges set aside while preparing the gravy.

METHOD FOR GRAVY

Heat wok and add one tablespoon of oil.

Fry onion until golden, then add the green

chillies, torn dry chillies, fenugreek seeds and fresh curry leaves and cook until aromatic.

Then add the rest of the ingredients except the curry powder and simmer gently until gravy is thick.

Now add the prepared omelettes, and sprinkle in special curry powder, while adding salt to taste.

Annasi Pineapple Curry

Annasi Pineapple Curry

INGREDIENTS

1 medium ripe pineapple, cleaned, peeled and diced into medium-size cubes
2 medium white onions or Spanish onions, diced
1 teaspoon turmeric powder
1 teaspoon cinnamon powder
1 stem lemongrass, bruised
2 sprigs of fresh curry leaves or 10 dry leaves
1½ cups coconut milk
1 teaspoon black mustard seeds, ground
1 teaspoon fennel seeds, roasted and powdered
6 dried chillies, powdered
4 tablespoons Sunflower oil
2 teaspoons sugar
Salt to taste

METHOD FOR OMELETTES

Place fennel seeds in a shallow frying pan over a low to medium heat and dry-roast seeds until lightly toasted and fragrant, allow to cool.

Place fennel seeds into a grinder and grind to a powder and set aside.

Repeat the above step with the dried chillies, roasting them until crispy and fragrant then allow them to cool, and grind coarsely.

Heat oil in a pan and fry onions until golden, adding lemon grass and curry leaves until fragrant.

Next add cut pineapple pieces, turmeric, mustard seeds, coarsely, ground chillies, sugar, salt and coconut milk and stir until all ingredients are well blended.

Reduce heat to low, cover and simmer for 10 minutes.

Remove from the heat and fold in the dry-roasted fennel powder.

Adjust seasoning according to taste.

This curry is best served with Mutton Pillau, Biriyani, Vegetable Pillau, Seafood and Meat Curries.

Brinjal Pahi

Brinjal Pahi

INGREDIENTS

4 medium-size eggplants cut lengthwise
into 2.5 cm finger strips
2 large white onions, thinly sliced
4 cloves garlic
2.5 cm piece ginger
1 teaspoon chilli powder
2 tablespoons black mustard seeds
1 tablespoon coriander seeds
1 teaspoon fennel seeds
1 teaspoon cumin seeds
6 banana capsicums, de-seeded and cut at
an angle
6 hot green chillies, cut lengthwise
1 teaspoon concentrated tamarind paste or
2 tablespoons tamarind pulp
2 tablespoons sugar
1 cup water
¼ cup white vinegar
Salt to taste
Sunflower oil for frying

METHOD

Heat oil in a deep frying pan and fry eggplant until golden brown, then remove and drain well on absorbent paper.

Combine ginger and garlic in a mortar and pound with 2 tablespoons of water to form a smooth paste (alternatively you can use a spice grinder) and set aside.

Dry-fry the coriander seeds, cumin seeds, fennel seeds and mustard seeds in a small frying pan over a low heat until the spices are fragrant and lightly toasted. Allow to cool, and then grind the spices to make a fine powder.

Transfer the powder to a saucepan with the ginger and garlic paste, vinegar, tamarind liquid, chilli powder, sugar and salt to taste, a cup of water and bring to the boil. Reduce heat and simmer until the sauce thickens, then allow to cool.

Adjust seasoning if necessary.

Before serving fold the sliced onions, capsicums and green chillies into the eggplants and pour the cooked sauce.

This dish is best served with Biriyani, Yellow Rice, Pillau or Vegetarian Curries.
NB: To make tamarind liquid, combine 1 part of tamarind paste with 3 parts of water and stir to form a liquid.

I do have a story to tell you regarding my friend Eva Gubacsi who I have known since 1985. She was fifteen years old when she walked into my Waves Café as a customer with her school friends. They would come regularly after school and have milkshakes and burgers. They used to tell me that we made the best milkshakes and burgers! One day she walked in on her own and asked me if I had a part-time job for her. I ended up offering her a job. She did not know what she was getting into, but was willing to give it a go. Eva had no idea about Asian food, let alone curries! Of course I had to train her through and there were some embarrassing moments! Don't get me wrong, she was an excellent waitress but when it came to describing the food... I once overheard her explaining about dhal to a customer, saying it was "this runny yellow stuff." Eva would never eat anything at the café. I used to tell her "just try the dhal..." Anyway, to cut a long story short, she said to me "I like it. I will try the dhal" and today, she eats the hottest curries with chillies and cooks her own beautiful curries as well.

Parippu - Dhal (Lentil Curry)

Parippu ~ Dhal (Lentil Curry)

INGREDIENTS (DHAL)

250 g Mysore dhal OR red lentils
1 medium white onion, finely diced
4 cloves garlic, finely chopped
2 green chillies, finely chopped
1 sprig fresh curry leaves
2 teaspoons coriander powder
1 teaspoon of cumin powder
1 teaspoon mustard seeds
2 dried chillies
2 tablespoons ghee
1 tin coconut milk
3 cups of water
Salt to taste

INGREDIENTS FOR GARNISH

Half a bunch of fresh coriander OR dill,
finely chopped cracked pepper

METHOD FOR DHAL

In a large bowl, wash and rinse lentils several times until the water is clear. Cover lentils with water and soak for 1 hour and drain.

Place drained lentils with 3 cups of water in a saucepan over a low heat and add turmeric, coriander, cumin powder, salt and stir. Gently cook, stirring occasionally, until lentils thicken.

Stir in coconut milk and simmer until dhal is soft and creamy.

Top with seasoning. (See below.)

SPINACH VARIATION

Once lentils thicken, fold in 1 bunch of shredded English spinach and simmer for 2–3 minutes. Then continue with the rest of the recipe.

METHOD FOR DHAL SEASONING

In a frying pan, heat ghee or oil and fry onions until golden.

Add torn dried chillies, fresh green chillies, mustard seeds and fresh curry leaves and sauté until aromatic.

When ready to serve, top dhal with this seasoning mixture and garnish with freshly grounded pepper, finely chopped coriander or dill leaves.

This dish is best served with meat, poultry and other vegetarian dishes.

Eggplant And Dry Fish Curry

Eggplant And Dry Fish Curry

INGREDIENTS

500 g eggplants, cut lengthwise into
5 cm thick slices
125 g dry salted Seer fish OR dry salted Tuna fish,
cut into cubes and soaked in cold water
1 medium white onion OR Spanish onion, finely
chopped
3 cloves garlic, finely sliced
2.5 cm piece green ginger, finely chopped
2.5 cm piece rampé (pandan leaf)
1 sprig fresh curry leaves
¼ teaspoon lemongrass, chopped
1 teaspoon turmeric powder
2 teaspoons coriander powder
1 teaspoon cumin powder
8 dried chillies OR 1 teaspoon hot chilli powder
½ teaspoon fenugreek seeds
1½ cups of coconut milk with equal parts of water
Juice of 1 lime
3 tablespoons Sunflower oil
Salt to taste

METHOD

Gently squeeze water from the pre-soaked fish cubes and set aside.

In a bowl, coat eggplant with turmeric and salt.

Heat oil in a heavy base saucepan over a medium heat and fry onions until golden.

Add garlic, ginger, fenugreek seeds, lemongrass, curry leaves, rampé and sauté until lightly toasted and fragrant.

Add coriander, cumin and chilli powder and mix through.

Gradually pour diluted coconut milk into the spices, while stirring.

Bring to the boil. Reduce heat, add eggplant slices and mix through until well coated with sauce. Cover and simmer for 20 minutes.

Add the dry fish and cook for further 10 minutes.

Add lime juice and salt to taste.

This dish complements boiled rice, Dhal, Green Mango Curry and Seafood Curries.

Green Mango Curry cooked with Palm Sugar is one of my Aunty Nahes' favourite dishes. The many years of growing up in her company taught me so many things. At the back of the kitchen was the washing area, and by the side was the built up grinding stone. Her Cooks, Ponan and Muthiah, would grind the spices daily for everyday cooking and it fascinated me. These days everything is so much easier! I want to share this mouth-watering fresh Mango Curry cooked with Palm Sugar. This dish could actually be called a chutney. It goes so well with any dish. If you are making this dish in Sri Lanka, you can substitute mangoes for the Umbrella fruit and follow the same recipe as shown above.

Green Mango Curry With Palm Sugar

Green Mango Curry With Palm Sugar

INGREDIENTS

4 medium unripe mangoes, peeled and
cut into thick slices
1 medium white onion, finely diced
2.5 cm piece fresh ginger, grated
2 teaspoons chilli powder
1 teaspoon turmeric powder
2 teaspoons mustard seeds
2 teaspoons coriander powder
1 teaspoon cumin powder
2 tablespoons of palm sugar, grated
¼ teaspoon lemongrass, finely chopped
1 sprig fresh curry leaves
2.5 cm piece rampé (pandan leaf)
2 cups coconut milk, diluted with equal
parts of water
2 tablespoons Sunflower oil
Salt to taste

METHOD

Heat oil in a wok over a low to medium heat and
fry onions until golden.

Add mustard seeds, ginger, curry leaves,
lemongrass and rampé and sauté until fragrant.

Gradually pour coconut milk into sautéed
ingredients.

Add coriander, cumin, chilli, turmeric powder and
salt to taste, then fold through until well-blended.

Bring sauce to the boil and when it begins to
thicken, reduce heat to low.

Gently fold in the sliced mango and palm sugar
and simmer until mango is softened.

NB: Fresh mangoes can be bought in many varieties and are available in Asian supermarkets or market stalls on weekends in the summer months.
Un-ripe mangoes are the most suitable for curries, chutney and pickles.

Green Banana ~ Ash Plantain Curry

Green Banana ~ Ash Plantain Curry

INGREDIENTS

2 large green bananas, available in produce
markets or Asian green grocers
1 large Spanish onion OR white onion, finely diced
2 green chillies cut lengthwise
1 sprig fresh curry leaves
1 stem lemongrass, thinly sliced
1 teaspoon turmeric powder
¼ teaspoon fenugreek seeds
2.5 cm stick cinnamon
1½ cups coconut milk, diluted with 2 cups of water
Juice of 1 lime
½ teaspoon of salt (to coat bananas)
Salt to taste

METHOD

Peel green bananas, cut in half lengthwise and
slice into 5 cm strips.

In a bowl, mix turmeric and salt together, then gently rub bananas with turmeric and salt and set aside.

In a heavy base saucepan over a low to medium
heat, place diluted coconut milk, fenugreek seeds,
onions, green chillies, fresh curry leaves, lemongrass and the cinnamon stick. Stir through and
gently bring sauce to the boil.

Gradually add sliced green banana and reduce heat
to low. Allow to simmer until bananas are tender.

Add lime and salt to taste. Remove from heat.

Serve this curry hot with Yellow Rice, Beef Badun, Dhal and Ginger Pachadi.

Vegetable Kofta Curry

After having worked in many restaurants and gained experience, I took another chance, as I wanted a break in life, so I bought a little business with my savings and a loan. I bought a café on Bondi Road, Sydney in 1985. As it was close to the beach, I called it "Waves". It was a very rundown café, so at first I made café style food, opening for breakfast and then I started to introduce spicy food into the menu. It became so popular that I went all out and changed the menu to all Sri Lankan food, and a few other dishes that I had learnt from past experiences. In no time people who lived around got to know about the place and I was working six nights a week.

Entrées like Potato Bonda brought back memories of the train ride to boarding school, so that was a must to have at Waves. It was one of my favourite vegetarian entrées at Shivahari's in the 70s. I remember a dish called 'The Vegetarian Plate' that consisted of five variations of curries, dhal, and vegetarian koftas made from two types of cheeses, riccotta and feta, which I deep-fried and cooked in pumpkin sauce. Another vegetarian curry was the Brinjal Pahi. In Sri Lanka, this dish is simmered in the sauce, but I always plated the eggplants with coloured capsicums and then poured hot sauce over them. For some reason it looks rustic and it added a distinct flavour to the dish. A vegetarian special of the day.

Vegetable Kofta Curry

INGREDIENTS (KOFTA)

250 g ricotta cheese
250 g feta cheese
1 cup plain flour
4 green chillies, de-seeded and finely chopped
½ teaspoon chilli powder
1 teaspoon cracked pepper
1 egg
Vegetable oil for frying

INGREDIENTS (CURRY SAUCE)

250 g butternut pumpkin
1 medium white onion, finely diced
1 teaspoon garlic, ground
1 teaspoon ginger, ground
1½ teaspoons chilli powder
2 tablespoons coriander powder
1 teaspoon cumin powder
1 teaspoon mustard seeds
1 sprig fresh curry leaves
1 teaspoon sugar
1 cup coconut milk, diluted with equal parts of water
4 tablespoons ghee
Sunflower oil for frying
Salt to taste

METHOD FOR KOFTA

Place ricotta and feta cheeses into a food processor or mix well in bowl until the cheese is well blended.

Add flour, chilli powder, cracked pepper, egg and mix through until well combined.

Rub some oil onto the palm of your hands before you begin to make the koftas.

Scoop a heaped tablespoon of the mixture and shape into 2.5 cm balls.

Place the balls on a lined tray.

Heat vegetable oil in a deep frying pan over medium heat.

Gently drop the cheese balls into hot oil and fry until golden.

Place on absorbent paper and allow to drain.

METHOD FOR CURRY SAUCE

Peel pumpkin, cut into large cubes and cover with water and cook till tender, then allow to cool.

In blender or food processor, blend pumpkin to a smooth pulp and set aside.

In a heavy base saucepan, heat ghee over a medium heat and fry onions until soft.

Add ginger, garlic, mustard seeds, coriander, cumin powder, curry leaves and sauté until spices are aromatic.

Stir in the pumpkin purée, diluted coconut milk, sugar and salt. Allow to simmer over a low heat for 15 minutes and remove from heat.

Before serving, gently add the koftas to the pumpkin sauce and simmer for 2–3 minutes.

Gently spoon the koftas onto a platter. (The koftas need to be handled delicately.)

When serving, pour warm pumpkin curry sauce over the koftas.

This dish is best served with vegetarian curries and Roti Channai.

Polos Ambul ~ Tender Jack Curry

Polos Ambul ~ Tender Jack Curry

INGREDIENTS

1 medium unripe jackfruit OR 4 tins young
jackfruit in brine (drained)
1 large white onion OR Spanish onion, finely diced
4 green chillies split lengthwise into strips
2 sprigs fresh curry leaves
2 tablespoons chilli powder
1 tablespoon roasted curry powder
1 teaspoon turmeric powder
5 cm stick cinnamon
1½ cups coconut milk, diluted with equal parts
of water
Juice of 1 lemon
2 tablespoons Sunflower oil
Salt to taste

INGREDIENTS FOR THE SEASONING

2 medium onions, finely chopped
1 sprig fresh curry leaves
2.5 cm piece lemongrass, thinly sliced
3 dried red chillies, cut into small pieces
1 teaspoon black mustard seeds
2 tablespoons Sunflower oil

METHOD

If using fresh unripe jackfruit, remove the thick
outer skin of the fruit, cut into cubes and marinate
in juice of lemon, then set aside.

If using young jackfruit in brine, drain the brine and
cut into cubes, then set aside.

Heat oil in a saucepan over medium to high heat.
Add onions, green chillies, fresh curry leaves and
sauté until onions are golden.

Add roasted curry powder, chilli powder and reduce
heat to low.

Fold in the fresh jackfruit and coat well with spice
mixture.

Stir in coconut milk and simmer until jackfruit is
tender, then remove from heat.

In a frying pan over a medium heat, heat oil and fry
onions until golden.

Add dry chillies, black mustard seeds and curry
leaves and fry until fragrant and chillies are crispy.

Add the seasoning to the cooked jackfruit curry and
stir through until well combined.

Serve hot with fluffy steamed rice.

N.B If you are using tinned jackfruit, make gravy until almost thick then add the jackfruit, at the very end.
This dish complements seafood curries and vegetarian dishes with steamed rice.

Chickpea And Potato Curry

Chickpea And Potato Curry

INGREDIENTS

250 g dried chickpeas OR 500 g canned
chickpeas (whole)
250 g potatoes cut into small cubes
1 large onion, finely chopped
6 green chillies, finely chopped
2.5 cm piece fresh ginger, finely chopped
½ cup coriander leaves
1 sprig fresh curry leaves
2 teaspoons coriander powder
1 teaspoon cumin powder
2½ teaspoons Garam Masala
3 ripe tomatoes, chopped finely
¼ cup tamarind pulp OR 1 tablespoon
lemon juice
2½ tablespoons ghee
2 teaspoons sugar
Salt to taste

METHOD

If using dried chickpeas, pre-soak overnight in cold water.

Place soaked chickpeas over a medium heat and boil until tender.

Drain and rinse chickpeas in cold water. Set aside. If using the canned chickpeas as a substitute, do not boil, (it will become overcooked and mushy) just add them at the end.

In a saucepan, boil cubed potatoes over a medium heat and cook until firm and tender. Drain and set aside.

Heat ghee in a heavy base pan over a medium heat and add onions, frying until golden.

Add chopped ginger and green chillies and fry until fragrant.

Stir in chopped tomatoes and curry leaves and cook until tomatoes are soft.

Add coriander, cumin powder and salt and stir through until the aroma of spices has heightened.

Fold in drained chickpeas and potatoes to the spices until well coated.

Stir through the Garam Masala and sugar.

Add the tamarind pulp or lemon juice. Slow cook for 10 minutes, stirring occasionally.

Serve hot and sprinkle with finely chopped fresh coriander leaves.

This dish complements vegetarian curries with steamed rice and accompanies Roti Channai and Chapati.

Ramani with her husband Vikram

I often travelled to India to visit my sister, Ramani. She left Sri Lanka in the late 60s to go to university in Madras. There she met her husband, Vikram. They married and settled in Chennai. We are very close and I use every chance I get to visit her. India fascinates me in many ways. It is a land of many traditions and contrasts. It is a land of beauty that offers experiences beyond the ordinary. A country known for a variety of spices, blends and flavours that can tickle any palate, whether it be at a street market stall or in a most prestigious restaurant.

I enjoyed spending quality time with her as we hardly spent much time together while growing up. We treasure every moment we spend together. We spend a lot of time talking about our childhood, schooldays, and our families. She had migrated to India at a young age and she missed out on learning the finer points of Sri Lankan cooking. When I was there we enjoyed sharing recipes of our homeland and Southern India. I am a great fan of Indian food. The food contains an array of spices that produce vibrant colours, textures and flavours. It is amazing to see the delicate spices and herbs come together to create dishes that are so distinct and unique. Ramani shared many recipes from the Southern States with me, which I have included in this cookbook.

In the mornings, Ramani would drive me to the market stalls to buy fresh vegetables, seafood or meat. On this particular morning we saw such a versatile purple eggplants that were small and rounded. There were so many varieties of eggplant at the market, but she chose these tender purple rounded ones and said she would teach me a special recipe that her mother-in-law had taught her. They had a cook called Kanniah who had worked in Vikram's home from when he was a teenager. He called it 'Ennai Katharikai', meaning 'oily eggplant'. He went to great trouble grinding the ingredients for making the masala. Fresh coconut is expensive in Chennai, in the state of Tamilnadu. Therefore it is always ground to a fine paste and used to get the desired texture to the dish. Many of the cooking customs and ideas come from various influences from neighbouring regions. A lot of onions, tomatoes are used in a curry to make it thick in the Southern states. Whereas in the North they use yoghurt, cashew nut paste in addition to the onions and tomatoes to achieve a thickness to the gravy or sauce.

Stuffed Eggplant Masala

Stuffed Eggplant Masala

INGREDIENTS

500 g round purple eggplants OR round green eggplants (Thai aubergines)
1 large white onion, finely chopped
4 cloves garlic, minced
2.5 cm piece fresh ginger, finely chopped
1 sprig fresh curry leaves
1 cup fresh coriander leaves, finely chopped
1 tablespoon chilli powder
1 teaspoon turmeric powder
1 tablespoon coriander seeds
2 teaspoons black mustard seeds
500 g ripe tomatoes, finely chopped
2 tablespoons Sunflower oil
½ cup freshly grated coconut OR desiccated coconut
2 cups water
Salt to taste

OKRA VARIATION

500 g long tender lady's fingers (Okra), seeds removed

METHOD

In a blender or grinder, combine coriander seeds, mustard seeds, ginger, garlic and coconut and make a smooth ground paste.

In a separate bowl, retain half of the ground paste to make the sauce.

Wash the eggplants and pat dry.

Using a sharp knife carefully cut the top end of eggplant and scoop out seeds. (Eggplants need to be hollow and seedless to fill with mixture.)

Place eggplants on a tray and fill with a heaped teaspoon of ground paste.

Heat oil in a heavy base saucepan over a medium heat and add onions and fry until golden brown.

Gradually add chopped tomatoes and curry leaves and cook until soft and tender.

Add the chilli and the turmeric powder and stir, adding the ground paste and fry until well combined.

Add water and salt and bring to the boil.
Reduce heat to low and add eggplants into sauce.

Spoon sauce over eggplant until well coated and allow eggplants to cook until tender. Simmer until sauce thickens, season with salt.

METHOD FOR THE OKRA VARIATION

If using okra, instead of eggplant, use a sharp knife and slit okra in the middle, remove seeds and fill with ground paste. Follow same method as above and cook until tender and firm. (Do not overcook lady's fingers, as they are tastier crunchy.) Make sure the vegetable retains its natural colour whilst cooking.

This dish complements vegetarian curries with steamed rice and accompanies Roti Channai and Chapati.

Cashew And Pea Curry

Cashew And Pea Curry

INGREDIENTS

500 g raw cashew nuts
2 white onions, finely diced
3 cloves garlic, thinly sliced
2.5 cm ginger, julienned
1 tablespoon chilli powder
1 teaspoon curry powder
1 teaspoon turmeric powder
250 g green peas, fresh OR frozen
4 green chillies, finely diced
400 ml coconut milk, diluted with
2 cups of water
Salt to taste

INGREDIENTS SEASONING

1 tablespoon Sunflower oil
½ teaspoon mustard seeds
A few sprigs fresh curry leaves
1 medium onion, finely diced

METHOD

Pre-wash the cashews and soak in water for 2 hours.

In a heavy base saucepan combine onions, ginger, garlic, chilli powder, curry powder, turmeric, fresh chillies and the coconut milk and cook over a low heat. Gently stir through until the sauce thickens.

Once sauce thickens, add green peas and cashew nuts and cook until tender. (Do not overcook the peas as they must be firm.)

Remove from heat and place in serving dish and garnish with seasoning.

METHOD FOR THE SEASONING

Heat oil in a saucepan over a medium heat and fry onions until golden.

Add mustard seeds, fresh curry leaves and sauté until infused and aromatic.

Arrange the seasoning over cashew curry.

Serve hot with rice.

This dish complements vegetarian curries with steamed rice and accompanies Roti Channai and Chapati.

Thakkali ~ Tomato Curry

Thakkali curry family recipe brought me back to my teenage year, a young school girl returning to boarding after school vacation during the 1960's. Mary our cook at that time used to prepare this dish for our train ride back to school. Delicately, Mary would wrap our dinner encased in a fresh banana leaf.I would unveil our "food parcel" to find string hoppers placed alongside the thakkali curry pol sambol, miris mallu and a boiled egg. As soon as the rain left the station, we would dig into our food no sooner the train left the station. The aroma would escape through the banana leaf making it irresistible to eat. Often fellow students travelling back to school experienced with memorable experience.

Thakkali ~ Tomato Curry

INGREDIENTS

1 kg ripe tomatoes, finely sliced
1 large white onion, finely diced
4 cloves garlic, ground to a paste
2.5 cm piece fresh ginger, ground
to a paste
6 hot green chillies, thinly sliced
1 sprig fresh curry leaves
2 tablespoons hot chilli powder
1 teaspoon turmeric powder
1 tablespoon sugar
2 tablespoons Sunflower oil
Salt to taste

METHOD

Slice tomatoes thinly and set aside.

Heat oil in a wok over a low to medium heat, add onions and fry until golden.

Add garlic, ginger, fresh curry leaves, sliced green chillies and sauté for a further 10 minutes.

Next, add turmeric, chilli powder and curry leaves cook until fragrant.

Add tomatoes and cook on high heat, stirring from time to time until all liquid is absorbed. Reduce heat to low adding salt and sugar to taste.

Gently simmer curry until it thickens and is rich in colour.

This flavoursome curry complements Roti Channai and Mutton Poriyal or String Hoppers and Prawn Curry or Cuttlefish Curry with rice. This sweet and tangy dish also accompanies vegetarian curries and can be served as a dip with flat breads.

White Potato Curry In Coconut Milk

White Potato Curry In Coconut Milk

INGREDIENTS

500 g waxy potatoes, peeled and
cut into cubes
1 tablespoon coriander powder
1 teaspoon turmeric powder
3 cloves garlic, finely chopped
2.5 cm fresh ginger, finely
chopped
1 large white onion, finely
chopped
3 green chillies, finely chopped
1 sprig fresh curry leaves
1 teaspoon fenugreek seeds
1 tin coconut milk
Juice of 1 lime
2 cups water
2 tablespoons Sunflower oil

METHOD

Heat oil in a heavy base saucepan and sauté onions until golden.

Add the fenugreek seeds, green chillies, fresh
curry leaves, garlic and ginger, and cook, stirring
often until softened and beginning to colour.

Add the peeled potatoes, turmeric and coriander
powder, and salt to taste.

Add water and coconut milk and simmer until
potatoes are tender and the gravy is fairly thick.

Add lime juice to taste.

This flavoursome curry complements Roti Channai and Mutton Poriyal or String Hoppers and Prawn Curry or Cuttlefish
Curry with rice. This sweet and tangy dish also accompanies vegetarian curries and can be served as a dip with flat breads.

Chilli Potatoes

Chilli Potatoes

INGREDIENTS

500 g potatoes, peeled, cut into 2 cm
cubes and covered with cold water
2 large white onions, thinly sliced
4 fresh green chillies, sliced lengthwise
1 tablespoon turmeric
½ teaspoon chilli powder
½ teaspoon chilli flakes
1 teaspoon mustard seeds
2 sprigs fresh curry leaves
2 cloves garlic, finely chopped
2.5 cm piece of fresh ginger, finely
chopped
Juice of ½ a lime
1 teaspoon salt
4 tablespoons ghee

METHOD

Place potatoes in a pan and bring to boil. Cook until
potatoes are half cooked and drain.

Heat ghee in a separate heavy base pot, sauté onions
until golden.

Add mustard seeds and fry, stirring until they crackle.

Add garlic, ginger, fresh curry leaves, green chillies,
chilli powder, turmeric and chilli flakes.

Cook, stirring until aromatic, then reduce heat.

Add potatoes and fold into fried spice mixture, stir fry
on low heat until potatoes are tender, adding salt and
lime juice to taste.

Murunga Curry ~ Drumstick Curry

Murunga Curry ~ Drumstick Curry

INGREDIENTS

500 g drumsticks (murunga), skinned and fibre removed
2 tablespoons curry powder
1 teaspoon turmeric powder
1 teaspoon chilli powder (optional)
1 teaspoon fenugreek seeds
1 large white onion OR Spanish onion, finely chopped
4 hot green chillies, sliced lengthwise
1 sprig fresh curry leaves
1½ tins coconut milk, diluted with equal parts of water
Juice of 1 lime
Salt to taste

METHOD

Cut the drumsticks (murunga) into 6 cm long pieces.

Wash and remove fibre from skin (you can leave the pieces whole or split them into two) and set aside.

Using a heavy base saucepan over a medium heat, combine turmeric, curry powder, chopped onions, green chillies, fresh curry leaves, chilli powder, fenugreek seeds, diluted coconut milk and cook, stirring occasionally.

Once the sauce begins to boil, reduce heat to low.

Add the drumsticks and gently stir and simmer for 15 minutes until tender and sauce is thick.

Add salt and lime juice to taste.

Serve hot.

METHOD FOR PRAWN VARIATION

If using prawns shell and de-vein 250 g green prawns and cook until tender, this is an authentic northern style curry. This dish complements other vegetarian and seafood curries and boiled rice.

NB: Drumsticks are available at many South Indian or Sri Lankan food stores.

Fish & Shellfish

Sura Varai

Sura Varai ~ Ling Fish Fry

INGREDIENTS

500 g Flake or Ling Fish
1 large white onion OR Spanish onion, finely chopped
1 teaspoon turmeric powder
2 teaspoons cumin seeds
1 tablespoon black peppercorns
3 dried red chillies, roughly broken
4 green chillies, finely chopped
1 cup freshly grated coconut OR desiccated coconut
Salt to taste
Juice of 1 lime
¼ cup Sunflower oil

METHOD

Cut fish into large portions.

In a medium saucepan, place fish, salt, turmeric and ½ cup of water and cook over a medium heat until fish is tender. Remove from heat.

Separate fish from the stock and retain stock for later.

Allow fish to cool and then flake fish until light and fluffy and set aside.

Grind cumin, peppercorns and coconut to a fine paste in grinder or with a mortar and pestle. Set aside.

Next, add ¼ cup of oil to a frying pan and heat over a medium heat and fry onions until golden and add torn dry chillies.

Add green chillies, fresh curry and fry until aromatic, adding coconut and the ground spice paste. Add flaked fish mixture, stirring until well coated.

Add in a little fish stock to the ingredients and stir fry on low heat until liquid is absorbed. Now add salt and lime juice to taste.

Serve as an accompaniment to rice and seafood curries.

PRAWN VARAI VARIATION

Cook prawns with salt, peppercorns and 1 teaspoon of turmeric powder in ½ cup of cold water for about 8 minutes. Follow the recipe as listed above.

This dish can also be made using Sea Bass, Cod or Gropper fishes.

Calamari Curry

Calamari Curry

INGREDIENTS

500 g Calamari (squid), cut into rings
1 large brown onion OR white onion, finely diced
4 cloves garlic, finely chopped
2.5 cm piece fresh ginger, finely chopped
6 green chillies, cut lengthwise
1 teaspoon fenugreek seeds
2.5 cm stem lemongrass
2 tablespoons chilli powder
1 tablespoon coriander powder
1 teaspoon turmeric powder
1 tablespoon special roasted curry powder
1 sprig fresh curry leaves
2 cm piece rampé (pandan leaf), cut into thin slices
1½ cups coconut milk
Juice of 1 lime
Salt to taste
2 tablespoons Sunflower oil

METHOD

Heat oil in a wok over a moderate heat and fry onion until golden brown.

Stir in ginger, garlic and sauté until fragrant.

Add rampé, lemongrass and fresh curry leaves and sauté until infused.

Add green chillies, chilli powder, turmeric powder, coriander and fenugreek seeds, then stir and cook for 3–4 minutes.

Gently stir in coconut milk, lime juice and salt to taste and gently simmer until the sauce reduces and thickens.

Over a high heat, gradually add calamari into the reduced sauce.

Stir in special dark roasted curry powder to coat calamari and simmer for 10 minutes.
(Do not overcook the calamari as it will become tough; it needs to be soft and tender.)

Coat the calamari sparingly with the sauce, as it is meant to be a dry curry.

This Northern Sri Lankan Calamari Curry is served with Prawn Pittu and Marci Sambal. It can also be served with String Hoppers and Turmeric Fish Curry or simply with steamed rice and Ginger Pachadi.

Fried Fish Curry ~ Northern Sri Lanka Fish Curry

Fried Fish Curry ~ Northern Sri Lanka Fish Curry

INGREDIENTS

500 g King Fish OR Spanish Mackerel cutlets
1 large white onion OR Spanish onion,
finely chopped
6 cloves garlic, peeled and cut lengthwise
2.5 cm piece fresh green ginger, thinly sliced
6 green chillies cut lengthwise into strips
1 teaspoon fenugreek seeds
2 sprigs fresh curry leaves
2.5 cm piece lemongrass, thinly sliced
6 dried chillies cut into 1 cm pieces
3 tablespoons chilli powder
1 teaspoon turmeric powder
2 tablespoons roasted curry powder
1 teaspoon concentrated tamarind pulp,
diluted with ¼ cup of water
1½ cups coconut milk, diluted with equal
parts of water
2 tablespoons olive oil OR vegetable oil
Sunflower oil for deep-frying
Salt to taste

METHOD

Cut fish cutlets into quarters, place in a bowl and rub well with turmeric and salt, then set aside.

Heat vegetable oil in a deep frying pan over a medium to high heat.

Once oil is hot, deep-fry fish until golden and crispy, allow it to drain on paper towel and set aside.

Heat 2 tablespoons of oil in a heavy base saucepan over a medium heat. Once oil is hot, add onion and fry until golden.

Add green chillies, garlic, ginger, fresh curry leaves, lemongrass, dried chillies, fenugreek seeds and sauté until ingredients are aromatic and the chillies have softened.

While stirring, add roasted curry powder and chilli powder and mix through until well blended. Continue to stir until spices have turned dark brown in colour.

Gradually pour in coconut milk and tamarind juice and stir.

Add salt and bring sauce to the boil, while stirring.

Reduce heat to low, add fried fish to the sauce and simmer for further five minutes

This Northern Sri Lankan curry is traditionally served with Eggplant and Dried Fish Curry, Ginger Pachadi, Sura Varai, Murunga Curry or boiled rice.

There are many beautiful dishes that my stepfather Wilmir Solomons enjoyed cooking, and one of my favourites was Fish Moilee. This is a very special dish that I was introduced to when he met my mum in the 1960s. He loved cooking and enjoyed teaching his 'hand-me-down' recipes from his mother, who was of Portuguese origin. He taught their Cook Wadduwe Ammae, from the Southern coastline of Sri Lanka this recipe.

Fish Moilee

Fish Moilee

INGREDIENTS

10 pieces King Fish OR Spanish Mackerel OR
Blue-Eyed Cod (cutlets)
2 large white onions, finely diced
5 cloves garlic, ground
2.5 cm piece fresh ginger, ground
8 green chillies, whole
2 sprigs fresh curry leaves
2 teaspoons turmeric
4 large ripe tomatoes, finely chopped
2 cups coconut milk OR 2 cups full cream milk
3 teaspoons plain flour
1 teaspoon vinegar
2 tablespoons Sunflower oil
Salt to taste

METHOD

In a heavy base saucepan, heat oil and fry onions over medium heat until golden.

Add whole green chillies to the onions and fry until softened.

Add tomatoes, turmeric, ginger, garlic and fresh curry leaves and sauté until tomatoes have softened.

In a jug, dissolve flour in a little coconut milk to make a smooth paste.

Gradually whisk in the rest of the coconut milk and set aside.

Pour the coconut milk mixture into the fried onion and tomato base.

Cook over a medium heat for 10 minutes, while stirring until the sauce slightly thickens.

Add the sliced fish pieces, vinegar and salt to taste and gently stir through.

Reduce heat and simmer for 8–10 minutes or until fish is cooked.

In Sri Lanka, Fish Moilee is often served with Yellow Rice, Kalu Pol and Pol Sambal.

Jaffna Style Crab Curry

Jaffna Style Crab Curry

INGREDIENTS

4 medium mud crabs
2 tablespoons chilli powder
1 teaspoon turmeric powder

INGREDIENTS (CURRY PASTE)

2 large brown onions OR white onions,
finely chopped
4 cloves garlic, finely chopped
2.5 cm piece fresh ginger, finely chopped
6 green chillies, de-seeded and finely chopped
1 teaspoon coriander seeds
1 teaspoon fenugreek seeds
1 teaspoon cumin seeds
1 teaspoon fennel seeds
1 teaspoon black peppercorns
1 sprig fresh curry leaves
2cm rampé OR pandan leaf
2 cups coconut milk
2 cups water
2 tablespoons scraped coconut OR
desiccated coconut
4 tablespoons special curry powder
Juice of 1 medium lime
Salt to taste

INGREDIENTS (GARNISH)

1½ cups murunga leaves OR 1 bunch fresh
coriander leaves

METHOD

Use a heavy base frying pan and dry - roast coriander, cumin, fennel seeds and black peppercorns, shaking the pan from side to side to form a crispy and crunchy texture, adding curry leaves and set aside.

Grind these ingredients into a fine paste using a spice grinder with enough water to make a thick paste and set aside.

In another pan, dry-roast the fresh or desiccated coconut until golden brown. Allow to cool.

Grind these ingredients into a paste by adding half a cup of water and set aside.

Wash and clean the crabs. Cut each crab into 6 pieces and set aside.

Bring coconut milk to the boil in a large saucepan, reduce heat.

Add the chopped onion, ginger, garlic, green chillies, lemongrass rampé, chilli and turmeric powder, and fenugreek seeds and stir.

Fold in the curry paste and coconut paste rapidly until all ingredients are well blended, bring the sauce to the boil adding the crab portions, and cook until the crab changes colour (approximately 15 minutes).

Sprinkle special roasted curry powder; add salt and lime juice to taste.

Finally add the coarsely chopped murunga or coriander leaves.

This traditional Jaffna Crab Curry is so rich in flavour and is eaten with steamed rice, Dhal, and Eggplant and Yoghurt Salad.

Prawn Curry

Prawn Curry

INGREDIENTS

1 kg large king prawns, peeled and de-veined
2 medium white onions, finely diced
4 cloves garlic, finely sliced
2.5 cm piece ginger, chopped
4 green chillies cut lengthwise
2.5 cm stem lemongrass, finely sliced
2 sprigs fresh curry leaves
2 teaspoons chilli powder
4 teaspoons coriander powder
2 teaspoons cumin powder
1 teaspoon fenugreek seeds
1 teaspoon turmeric
2 cups coconut milk, diluted with 1 cup of water
Juice of 1 lime
3 tablespoons Sunflower oil
Salt to taste

METHOD

Heat oil in a pan and fry the onions over medium heat until golden.

Add garlic, ginger, curry leaves, lemongrass, and green chillies and stir to combine.

Add the fenugreek seeds and fry until fragrant.

Stir in the coriander powder, cumin powder, chilli powder and turmeric powder and cook over medium heat until aromatic.

Gently pour in the diluted coconut milk, lime juice and salt and bring the sauce to the boil over a low to medium heat.

Add the prawns and simmer very gently for 8 minutes.

Serve with Yellow Rice, Thakkali Curry, Brinjal Pahi or Tomato and Onion Sambal.

Sura Curry ~ Ling (Fish Curry)

Sura Curry ~ Ling (Fish Curry)

INGREDIENTS

500 g Ling fillets cut into small cubes
1 large Spanish onion, finely chopped
10 green chillies cut into small pieces
3 tablespoons chilli powder
1 teaspoon turmeric
2 tablespoons special roasted curry powder
1 teaspoon fenugreek seeds
1 tablespoon tamarind pulp
1½ cups coconut milk, diluted with equal parts of water
1 sprig curry leaves
Juice of 1 large lime
Salt to taste

METHOD

Cut Ling fillets into bite-size cubes and set aside.

Heat a heavy base saucepan over a medium heat.

Pour diluted coconut milk, chilli powder turmeric and tamarind pulp into heated pan, and stir over medium heat.

Add onions, fresh curry leaves, green chillies, ginger, garlic and fenugreek.

Stir through until well combined and cook until ingredients are soft and aromatic.

Gradually add the fish and stir, adding curry powder, salt and lime juice to taste.

Allow to cook for 10–12 minutes.

Sura Curry is a Northern Sri Lankan dish, which is traditionally served with Pittu. It can also be served with boiled rice, Murunga Curry, Crab Sambal and Marci Sambal. This dish can also be made using Sea Bass, Cod or Gropper fishes.

Fish Sarakku Curry

INGREDIENTS

500 g King Fish or Spanish Mackerel,
cut into quarters
1 medium white or Spanish onion,
finely chopped
6 cloves garlic, cut in halfs
2.5 cm piece ginger, thinly sliced
4 green chillies, finely chopped
2 tablespoons Sarakku Thull
1 teaspoon fenugreek seeds
1 tablespoon tamarind pulp
1 cup grated fresh coconut OR
desiccated coconut
2¼ cups water
Salt to taste

METHOD

In a frying pan, dry-roast the coconut over a medium heat until golden.

In a grinder, place the roasted coconut and grind whilst gradually adding ¼ cup of water to form a fine paste (if necessary, continue to add a little more water to achieve desired consistency) and set aside.

Place fenugreek seeds in a heavy base pan over a medium heat and dry-roast until fenugreek turns brownish yellow.

Use a heavy bottom saucepan; add 2 cups of water, onions, garlic, ginger and green chillies, roasted fenugreek seeds and Sarakku Thull.

Stir through and bring to the boil.

Next, add the roasted coconut paste, tamarind and salt and stir until well combined.

Add the fish quarters and stir.

Reduce heat to low and cook for 10 minutes.

This traditional dish is not only flavoursome but is nutritious and can be served with Rasam, Eggplant, Prawn Curry and country rice (red) or white rice.

Fish Cooked In Banana Leaf

INGREDIENTS

500 g whole Snapper OR Red Mullet
3–4 shallots
½ teaspoon garlic, ground
2.5 cm piece ginger, ground
1 teaspoon red chillies, finely chopped
3–4 curry leaves, finely chopped
¼ teaspoon turmeric powder
Juice of 1 lime
2 tablespoons olive oil OR coconut oil
Salt to taste
2 large kebab sticks OR satay sticks
1 large banana leaf

METHOD

Ensure the fish is properly scaled and cleaned.

Using a sharp knife, make large 2.5 cm slits running along both sides of the fish (so the fish can absorb the marinade) and set aside.

Combine chillies, turmeric, curry leaves, shallots, ginger, garlic, salt and lime in a grinder or mortar and pestle and grind to form a coarse paste.

Generously apply a thick layer of the paste to coat the inside and outside of the fish.

Place the banana leaf on a lightly oiled frying pan over a medium heat (to make it pliable to wrap fish).

Remove from pan and place on a tray or bench.

Carefully wrap the fish in the banana leaf, securing all sides with a kebab stick.

Heat oil in a large frying pan, over a medium heat. Place the wrapped fish onto the heated pan and slow cook on each side for 8–10 minutes.

NB: You can also cook this dish by wrapping it in baking paper to form a parcel by securing all sides tightly, so that juices don't escape. Add an extra tablespoon of oil to the grounded paste to retain moisture. Bake in moderate oven for 20 minutes.

I had the opportunity to learn deep southern style of cooking, at my then sister-in-law Norma Pereira's home in Galle. Her amme (cook), Hinnihami, was a loving betel chewing cherubic character. For her cooking Miris Malu (Chilli Fish) was kind of a ritual. She used to grind the curry paste for this dish and it was indeed a laborious task, but the taste was surely a thing to die for! Though the fish was purchased from an open air rustic looking market, it used to be of the finest quality. This dish was cooked in clay pots on an open fire. This hot peppery fish dish is awesome with Hoppers, Kiri Bath and Steamed Rice. It was a delight for me to have fine-tuned my Sinhalese style cooking at Norma's house.

Miris Mallu

INGREDIENTS

500 g Tuna OR King Fish OR Spanish Mackerel
1 large white onion, finely diced
4 cloves garlic, finely chopped
2.5 cm piece ginger, ground
2 green chillies split lengthwise
2.5 cm piece rampé leaf OR pandan leaf
1 sprig curry leaves
1 teaspoon coriander seeds
1 teaspoon fennel seeds
1 teaspoon cumin seeds
1 teaspoon fenugreek seeds
2.5 cm stick cinnamon
1 tablespoon chilli powder
1 teaspoon turmeric powder
1 teaspoon black peppercorns
1 teaspoon Goraka (Gamboge)
4 cups water
Salt to taste

METHOD

Cut fish into medium-size portions and set aside.

In a grinder, add coriander, cumin, peppercorns and blend to a smooth powder. Set aside.

In a food processor, add onions, ginger, garlic, chilli powder, Goraka and turmeric and blend to form a fine paste.

In a heavy base saucepan, bring 4 cups of water to the boil.

Add fresh curry leaves, lemongrass, fenugreek seeds, onion paste and ground spices.

Stir through and cook over a moderate heat for 10 minutes.

While stirring, add salt to taste and bring to the boil.

Lastly, add fish portions, reduce heat to low and allow it to simmer for 8–10 minutes.

Putti Aachie's Prawn Thiyal

Putti Aachie's Prawn Thiyal

INGREDIENTS

750 g raw medium prawns, peeled and de-veined
150 g desiccated coconut OR fresh coconut, scraped
2 large white onions, finely chopped
4 cloves garlic, finely chopped
5 cm piece rampé or pandan leaf
2.5 cm piece lemongrass, finely chopped
1 sprig fresh curry leaves
4 green chillies, finely chopped
1 teaspoon fenugreek seeds
1 teaspoon turmeric powder
1 tablespoon black peppercorns
2 tablespoons coriander powder
1 tablespoon cumin powder
1 teaspoon chilli powder
3 tablespoons Sunflower oil
50 g tamarind, dissolved in ½ cup of water
Salt to taste

METHOD

In a heavy base frying pan, dry-roast coconut until it gets a rich golden colour and set aside to cool.

Place coconut in a grinder or a food processor and blend until smooth by adding a little water.

Dry-roast black peppercorns, then add coriander, cumin powder and roast lightly until they change colour and are fragrant. Then set them aside.

Add these spices to the ground coconut paste and grind until all ingredients are well blended.

Heat oil in a heavy base saucepan over medium heat, then add onions and fry until golden.

Add green chillies, ginger and garlic and cook until aromatic.

Add fenugreek seeds, curry leaves, pandan leaves and lemongrass and cook over low heat until transparent.

Add the ground coconut and spice mixture, chilli and turmeric powder and stir well.

Reduce heat to low and add 300 ml of hot water and cook, until gravy has thickened and almost dry, add the prawns and tamarind pulp and cook for further 6-8 minutes.

(Do not overcook the prawns as they become too rubbery; they should be succulent and tender to eat.) This curry is great with Vegetable Pillau Rice, Mango and Palm Sugar, Chilli Potatoes or Eggplant and Onion Sambal.

Fish And Green Mango Curry

Fish And Green Mango Curry

INGREDIENTS

500 g Spanish Mackerel, cut into 3 cm pieces
2 tablespoons chilli powder
1 teaspoon turmeric powder
2 medium white onions, finely chopped
4 cloves garlic, thinly sliced
2.5 cm piece fresh ginger, thinly sliced
1 teaspoon fenugreek seeds
3 small green chillies
1 sprig fresh curry leaves
1 tablespoon coriander powder
2 teaspoons cumin powder
400 ml coconut milk
1 cup water
2 fibrous green mangoes, sliced lengthwise
3 tablespoons Sunflower oil
Salt to taste

METHOD

Place the chilli, coriander and cumin in a frying pan and dry-roast over low heat until aromatic. Set aside to cool.

Grind the above spices by adding a little water, to form a smooth paste.

Heat oil in a heavy base saucepan over medium heat and fry onions until golden.

Add ginger, garlic, fenugreek seeds, fresh curry leaves, and green chillies and cook until fragrant.

Add lemongrass and sliced mangoes, salt and turmeric.

Stir in blended spices and coconut milk and simmer for 10 minutes.

When mango is almost tender and gravy is thick, add sliced fish and cook for a further 8 minutes.

Squid Stuffed With Green Prawns Jaffna Style

Squid Stuffed With Green Prawns Jaffna Style

INGREDIENTS

8 medium squid tubes
250 g peeled green prawns (raw), minced coarsely
1 teaspoon turmeric powder
1 teaspoon coarse black peppercorns
2½ teaspoons coriander powder
1 teaspoon cumin powder
2 teaspoons chilli powder
1 teaspoon fenugreek seeds
2 tablespoons special dark roasted curry powder
(see recipe page 84)
1 large white onion, finely chopped
2 teaspoons ginger, freshly grated
2 large red chillies, de-seeded and finely chopped
4 cloves garlic, finely chopped
2 sprigs fresh curry leaves
2.5 cm piece lemongrass, thinly sliced
Juice of 1lime
400 ml coconut milk
2 cups cold water
2 tablespoons Sunflower oil
Salt to taste

STUFFING FOR SQUID

1 large Spanish onion, finely chopped
2 cm piece fresh ginger, finely chopped
2 hot green chillies, finely chopped
2 cloves garlic, finely chopped
2 teaspoons black peppercorns, coarsely ground
1 teaspoon chilli powder
1 teaspoon salt

PREPARING THE SQUID

Clean the squid under running water.
Remove inner quill and pull away head and tentacles,
then cut tentacles, pulling off the skin and washing
squid thoroughly. Finely chop the
tentacles and set aside.

Bring 8 cups of water to the boil in a saucepan.
Add a teaspoon of salt and drop the squid tubes into
the water and cook for 5 minutes.
Strain stock and retain juices for curry sauce.

METHOD

Into the minced green prawns, add squid tentacles,
onion, ginger, garlic, pepper, chilli powder, green chillies
and salt and mix well until well combined.

Fill squid with prepared stuffing, securing the opening
with wooden picks. Set aside while preparing the sauce.

Heat oil in a heavy base pan, add chopped onions and
fry until golden.

Next add ginger, garlic, green chillies, fresh curry leaves
and lemongrass and stir-fry for a minute.

Add fenugreek seeds and toast until it has a nutty aroma.

Add the coriander, cumin, turmeric and chilli powder,
and stir through until aromatic.

Add squid stock and stir through until all ingredients are
well blended.

When the sauce begins to thicken, add the coconut milk
along with water and bring it to a boil, then simmer.

Add the stuffed squid tubes and cook for 10–15 minutes
or until just cooked through.

Sprinkle special roasted curry powder and add lime
juice to taste.

Remove from heat and serve.

My great grandmother Ponamma
My aunty Pathmini
My cousin Shantha

Amma and I love talking about my great grandmother Ponnamma, who was a great cook. My mum shared many recipes with me that she was able to learn from her while growing up.

My great grandmother lived in a village called Manipay in the Northern part of Sri Lanka. One of her favourite dishes was the Aubergine and Prawn curry cooked in coconut milk.

Amma says that her Aachie (grandma) used to make the scrumptious dish for her which I am sharing with you. All these dishes came from a very simple kitchen. In those days there were no gas stoves, or electric hot plates, but it was a cook top made from clay and fire wood was used for preparing the dishes. The vegetable vendor would arrive at the front door and Ponnamma would select the best purple rounded eggplants which she marinated in turmeric and salt. Mum said the fish and prawns had great flavour which was bought at the front gate. Her maid Annapillai was just a young girl then, who used to help her prepare all the ingredients so that Ponnamma could cook up a feast.

To make the eggplant and prawn curry dish Ponnamma lightly roasted the spices and then they were ground on the grinding stone to a fine paste. Mum says that she used to tell her that she liked using freshly scraped coconut which was ground to a smooth paste as it gave more texture to the curries and also because she did not have to use too much of it, rather than use coconut milk. She always cooked her curries in clay pots, first she sauteed the spices, then gradually added the coconut paste mixing through adding enough water to make the sauce and cooked the eggplants and lastly adding the prawns.

Eggplant And Prawn Curry

Eggplant And Prawn Curry

INGREDIENTS

500g eggplants cut lengthwise
into 5 cm thick slices
250 grams of fresh green prawns
cleaned and deveined
1 medium white onion OR Spanish
onion, finely chopped
3 cloves garlic, finely sliced
2.5 cm piece green ginger, finely
chopped
1 sprig fresh curry leaves
1 teaspoon turmeric powder
2 teaspoons coriander powder
1 teaspoon cumin powder
1 teaspoon hot chilli powder
1 teaspoon fenugreek seeds
1½ cups of coconut milk with
equal parts of water
Juice of 1 lime
3 tablespoons Sunflower oil
Salt to taste

METHOD

In a bowl, coat eggplant with turmeric and salt.

Squeeze excess water from the eggplant, and set aside.

Heat oil in a heavy base saucepan over a medium heat and fry onions until golden.

Add garlic, ginger, fenugreek seeds, curry leaves, until lightly toasted and fragrant.

Add coriander, cumin and chilli powder and mix through.

Gradually pour diluted coconut milk into spices, whilst stirring.

Bring to the boil. Reduce heat, add eggplant slices and mix through until well coated with sauce. Cover and simmer for 20 minutes.

When eggplant is almost tender, add the cleaned prawns, and cook until succulent.

Add lime juice and salt to taste.

Complements boiled rice, tomato curry, chilli potatoes and seafood curries.

Coastal Fish Curry

INGREDIENTS

1 kg King Fish OR Spanish Mackerel cutlets
1 large white onion, finely chopped
4 cloves garlic, thinly cut
2.5 cm piece fresh ginger, thinly sliced
3 green chillies split lengthwise
2.5 cm stem lemongrass, thinly sliced
1 sprig fresh curry leaves
3 teaspoons chilli powder
1 teaspoon turmeric powder
1 teaspoon fenugreek seeds
2 cups coconut milk
1 cup water
Sunflower oil for frying
Juice of 1 lime
Salt to taste

METHOD

Cut fish cutlets into quarters and set aside.

Heat vegetable oil in a heavy base saucepan over a medium heat add onions and fry until golden then add ginger, garlic, fresh curry leaves, lemongrass, green chillies and sauté until chillies have softened.

While stirring, add chilli powder, turmeric and fenugreek and cook until fragrant reducing the heat.

Gradually pour in coconut milk and water, and almost bring to the boil.

Add the fish quarters and cook for 10 minutes.

Season with lime juice and salt according to taste.

MILD VARIATION

For a milder Fish Curry omit the chilli powder and add an additional teaspoon of turmeric powder when preparing and you will have a delicious mild creamy curry.

Fish Curry is a well-known seafood dish throughout Sri Lanka and is often served for breakfast with String Hoppers, Hoppers and Kiri Bath, this curry is also splendid with Thakkali Curry, Raal Appam and boiled rice.

Meat & Poultry

Lamb Korma

Lamb Korma

INGREDIENTS

1.25 kg boned leg of lamb
2 tablespoons cumin seeds
2 teaspoons chilli powder
1 tablespoon black peppercorns
1 teaspoon turmeric powder
2.5 cm cinnamon stick
6 cardamom pods
5 cloves
6 hot green chillies
4 white onions, thinly sliced
250 g ripe tomatoes, finely chopped
6 cloves garlic, finely chopped
2.5 cm fresh root ginger, finely chopped
1 bunch fresh coriander leaves, finely chopped
¼ cup ghee
1 cup mint leaves, finely chopped
4 tablespoons coriander seeds
1 cup creamy yoghurt, beaten lightly

METHOD

Trim fat from lamb and cut into 3 cm cubes.

Dry-roast the coriander, cumin seeds and peppercorns in a frying pan on medium heat until fragrant.

Allow to cool and grind to a fine powder.

Grind ginger and garlic to a fine paste and set aside.

Grind cinnamon, cardamom and cloves coarsely.

Marinate meat in yoghurt, turmeric, chilli powder and ground spices and set aside while you prepare the rest of the ingredients.

Heat ghee in a heavy base pan and when oil is hot add onions and fry until golden.

Add finely chopped tomatoes and green chilli, cook until soft, then stir in the ginger and garlic paste and cook until aromatic.

Keep stirring the mixture and fry until it changes colour.

Add the marinated lamb and mix through the spice mixture and cook over a medium to low heat for 50 minutes, stirring from time to time.

Add finely chopped coriander leaves, mint leaves and salt to taste.

Lamb Korma is a warm mild to medium dish and complements Yellow Rice, Prawn Curry, Tomato Curry and Mixed Vegetable Pickle.

I would go in the kitchen and watch Wadduwe Ammac make her many delicious dishes like this one, my favourite was the Pork Kalupol with dry-roasted rice and coconut, she would make it for Sunday lunch with yellow white potato curry rice, and other accompaniments that went together.

Kalu Pol Curry ~ Blackened Coconut Pork

Kalu Pol Curry ~ Blackened Coconut Pork

INGREDIENTS

1 kg of shoulder pork, cut into cubes
1 large white onion, finely diced
4 cloves garlic, finely chopped
2.5 cm piece ginger, ground
2.5 cm piece rampé (pandan leaf)
2.5 cm stem lemongrass
2 tablespoons coriander seeds
1 tablespoon cumin seeds
1 teaspoon fenugreek seeds
1 tablespoon fennel seeds
1 tablespoon black peppercorns
4 cardamom pods
4 cloves
2.5 cm stick cinnamon
20 hot red chillies, dried
½ cup white vinegar
1 cup freshly grated coconut OR desiccated coconut
¼ cup of raw rice, red country OR white rice
2¼ cups water
3 tablespoons Sunflower oil
Salt to taste

METHOD

Cut pork into cubes, marinate in turmeric and salt, and set aside.

Place coriander, cumin, fenugreek, fennel seeds, black peppercorns, cardamom, cloves and cinnamon in a pan over a low heat.

Dry-roast spices, shaking the pan or tossing the spices so they don't scorch. Allow to roast until the aroma of the spices has heightened (as an indicator, the aroma of the coriander should smell sweet, cumin is nutty, the fenugreek changes to a subtle brownish-yellow colour).

Place cooled dry-roasted spices in a grinder or blender, grind to a fine powder and set aside.

In a heavy base pan over a low to medium heat, dry-roast coconut until rich golden brown then place in a bowl and allow it to cool.

Place rice in the same pan and toast until dark golden in colour, and then allow it to cool.

Combine the toasted rice, coconut and ¼ cup of water and grind until it forms a thick paste. (Add extra water if necessary, to reach desired consistency.)

Heat oil in heavy base saucepan over a medium heat.

When oil is hot, add onions and fry until golden then add ground ginger and garlic and sauté.

Mix through fresh curry leaves lemongrass and pandan leaves, and continue to fry until aromatic.

Add the grounded spices and fry until dark brown in colour.

Gently fold in diced pork and coat well with spice mixture.

Mix in the rice and coconut paste until all ingredients are well combined.

Add the vinegar, salt and remaining water, stir through and reduce heat to low stirring from time to time and cook curry for 45 minutes or until tender.

(The sauce should be thick and dark brown in colour.)

This curry, rich in flavours, is best served as a meal accompanied with Yellow Rice, Chilli Potatoes, Roll Cutlets and Brinjal Pahi. It is also a dish that presents well, simply on its own or with South East Asian flat bread.

Pork Sorpotel

Pork Sorpotel

INGREDIENTS

750 g lean pork neck OR shoulder pork
250 g lamb's liver OR calf's liver
1 large white onion, finely chopped
12 cloves garlic, finely chopped
2.5 cm piece ginger, finely ground
5 green chillies, finely chopped
1 sprig fresh curry leaves
1 teaspoon turmeric powder
2 tablespoons coriander seeds
1 tablespoon cumin seeds
1 tablespoon black mustard seeds
4 cardamom pods
4 cloves
1 small stick cinnamon
12 red (deep red) chillies, dried
1½ tablespoons tamarind pulp, dissolved
with ½ cup of water
3 tablespoons olive oil
¾ cup of vinegar
Salt to taste
2 tablespoons ghee

METHOD

Trim skin from pork and cut into large portions.

Place pork into a heavy base saucepan over a low heat and dry-fry, turning over with tongs.

Allow to lightly brown to expel the pork juices and remove from heat.

Drain pork, retaining any remaining juices in a separate bowl and allow it to cool.

Place the livers in a medium saucepan, adding water to cover them.

Simmer over a medium to low heat for 10 minutes until livers are tender.

Drain and retain juices separately and allow to cool, set it aside.

Place the coriander, cumin seeds, black peppercorns, cardamom, cloves, dried chillies and cinnamon in a pan over low heat.

Dry-roast the spices, shaking or tossing the pan so that the spices don't scorch.

Allow to roast until golden and the aroma of the spices is heightened (as an indicator, the aroma of the coriander should smell sweet and cumin is nutty) then allow it to cool.

Place dry-roasted spices in a grinder or blender, grind to a fine powder and set aside.

Cut the pork and liver portions into small cubes and set aside.

Heat ghee in a heavy bottom pan over a medium heat and fry onions until golden.

Add ginger, garlic, green chillies, curry leaves and sauté until fragrant.

Add cooked pork, livers and turmeric powder and fry until the meat has turned a rich brown colour.

Sprinkle roasted curry powder over the pork and liver and mix through.

Gradually pour tamarind, vinegar, and retained pan juices and stir through until well combined.

Season with salt, according to taste.

Bring the curry to the boil and then reduce heat to low and simmer for 20 minutes or until the meat is tender, stirring occasionally.

Serve this rich and spicy Goan Curry with Mutton Pillau, Cashew and Pea Curry, and Brinjal and Yoghurt Salad.

Pork Vindaloo

The Vindaloo style of cooking originated on India's West coast, in Kerala and its neighbouring states, and its style spread into Portuguese influenced Goa. This is another dish the De Souza's shared with me before they took over Shivahari's in the late 1970s. Mrs. De Souza had told me that a Vindaloo Curry should be cooked a few days ahead, so it allows the meat to soften and that the slightly harsh taste of freshness is reduced in this tangy dish.

Pork Vindaloo

INGREDIENTS

1 kg shoulder pork OR leg pork
1 large white onion, finely chopped
6–8 cloves garlic
2.5 cm piece fresh ginger, finely chopped
2 bay leaves
1 teaspoon turmeric powder
¼ cup coriander seeds
1 tablespoon cumin seeds
6 cloves
2.5cm piece stick cinnamon
2 tablespoons black peppercorns
20 hot red chillies, dried
¼ cup white vinegar OR malt vinegar
2 cups beef stock
3 tablespoons ghee
Salt to taste

METHOD FOR CURRY PASTE

Place the coriander, cumin seeds, black peppercorns, cloves, dried chillies and cinnamon in a pan over a low to medium heat.

Dry-roast the spices for 3–4 minutes, while continuously shaking the pan or tossing the spices so they don't scorch.

Allow to roast until spices are golden and the aroma is heightened (as an indicator, the aroma of the coriander should smell sweet and the cumin is nutty and chillies softened and puffed up) then allow it to cool.

Place dry-roasted spices in a grinder.

Pulse grind while gradually adding vinegar to form a fine paste and set aside.

METHOD FOR CURRY

Trim and cut meat into medium-size cubes.

Marinate meat with the prepared curry paste for at least 2 hours.

In a blender or grinder, place onions, garlic, ginger and turmeric, and blend until it forms a fine paste, then set aside.

Heat ghee in a heavy base saucepan over medium heat and fry onion paste until golden.

Add bay leaves, marinated pork and salt and fold through until well coated.

Gradually pour stock over meat and stir through until well combined.

Cover and gently simmer over a low heat for 1½ hours, stirring occasionally until meat is tender.

Serve this aromatic curry with Basmati rice and Pudina Chutney.

Wok-Fried Pork With Banana Chilli And Spanish Onions

Wok-Fried Pork With Banana Chilli And Spanish Onions

INGREDIENTS

500 g pork fillet, thinly sliced
250 g Spanish onions, thinly sliced
1½ teaspoons garlic, crushed
1½ teaspoons ginger, crushed
6 banana chillies, de-seeded and sliced
angularly
6 Thai red chillies, finely chopped
1 teaspoon dry chilli flakes
1½ teaspoons brown sugar
1½ tablespoons light soya sauce
1½ tablespoons dark soya sauce
1 tablespoon sesame oil
2 tablespoons peanut oil
Salt to taste

METHOD

Slice pork thinly into narrow strips.

Rub pork with salt, garlic, ginger and chilli flakes allow to marinate for 30 minutes.

Heat sesame and peanut oil in wok over a high heat, toss in red chillies and fry until crispy.

Add the marinated pork and stir-fry until meat is brown.

Add brown sugar, sliced onions, banana chillies, light and dark soya sauce and salt to taste.

Stir-fry continuously until meat is coated well with ingredients. Cook until meat is tender.

Remove from heat and serve.

Serve this dish with egg noodles or fluffy white rice.

Devilled Pork

Devilled Pork

INGREDIENTS

750 g leg pork OR shoulder pork
1 large onion, sliced thinly
3–4 cloves garlic, finely chopped
5 cm piece ginger, finely chopped
1 stalk lemongrass, grated
8–10 hot red chillies, dried
1 teaspoon turmeric powder
3 teaspoons black mustard seeds
8 raw cashew nuts, whole
2 teaspoons sugar
1¼ cup chicken stock
1 tablespoon soya sauce
2 tablespoons vinegar
3 tablespoons Sunflower oil
Salt to taste

METHOD

Trim pork, cut into cubes and place in a bowl.

Marinate pork with soya sauce and vinegar and set aside for 2 hours to tenderise.

In a grinder, place red chillies, mustard seeds and cashew nuts and grind to a smooth paste. Set aside.

Next grind ginger and garlic to a fine paste.

In a heavy base saucepan over a medium heat, add oil and fry onions until golden.

Add the ginger and garlic paste to the onions and continue to fry for 3–4 minutes until fragrant.

Add ground chilli, mustard and cashew paste and stir through until all ingredients are well blended.

Fold in the marinated pork and coat well with mixture.

Gradually pour chicken stock, grated lemongrass, sugar and salt to taste.

Stir and cover, then gently simmer for 45 minutes until pork is tender.

Uncover saucepan and allow liquid to be absorbed, leaving a thick sauce to coat meat.

Remove from heat when sauce is reduced and becomes dry.

Serve hot with a meal of basmati rice, Chilli Potatoes, Dhal, Tomato Sambal or Dry Fish and Onion Sambal.

Mutton Poriyal

Mutton Poriyal

INGREDIENTS

1 kg mutton off the bone
1 large white onion, finely diced
6 cloves garlic, finely chopped
2.5cm piece ginger, ground
2.5 cm stem lemongrass, sliced
2.5 cm rampé, finely chopped
1 sprig fresh curry leaves
2 teaspoons chilli powder
1 teaspoon turmeric powder
1 tablespoon fennel seeds
1 tablespoon coriander seeds
1 teaspoon cumin seed
1 teaspoon fenugreek seeds
6 cardamoms pods
6 cloves
1 small cinnamon stick
1 teaspoon black peppercorns
2 cups coconut milk
6 medium potatoes cut into
small to medium-size cubes
Lemon juice OR lime juice to taste
3 tablespoons ghee
Salt
Oil for frying potatoes

METHOD

Dice mutton or lamb into small to medium size cubes.

In a bowl, mix in turmeric, salt and chilli powder to marinate meat.

Allow to chill in the refrigerator for one hour.

In a heavy base pan, over a medium heat, add fennel, coriander, cumin, black peppercorns, cinnamon, cardamom and cloves.

Dry-roast the spices for 3–4 minutes, while continuously shaking the pan or tossing the spices, so they don't scorch. Allow to roast until spices are dark in colour and the aroma is heightened. (As an indicator, the aroma of the coriander should smell sweet and cumin is nutty.)

Allow spices to cool, then place into a grinder and grind to a fine powder.

Peel potatoes and cut into small cubes.

In a deep pan, heat vegetable oil and fry potatoes until crisp and golden.

Drain on absorbent paper and set aside.

Using a heavy base saucepan, heat ghee and fry onions until golden over a medium heat.

Add ginger, garlic, fresh curry leaves, lemongrass, rampé, fenugreek seeds and sauté until aromatic.

Mix in the marinated meat and stir until all ingredients are well combined.

Stir in coconut milk and increase heat to high.

Allow meat to cook, while stirring, until almost tender and sauce is reduced to a thick consistency.

Mix in 2 heaped tablespoons of the ground roasted curry powder to coat meat, and cook for further 10 minutes.

Add lime juice or lemon juice, salt to taste and cook until curry is almost dry, and fold in the fried potatoes.

(This is a dry curry where the meat is coated with fragrant and exotic spices.)

Mutton Poriyal is a Northern Sri Lankan dish traditionally served with String Hoppers, Roti Channai, Mutton Pillau and Yellow Rice. Other accompanying dishes include Brinjal Pahi or Mango Curry with Palm Sugar. As this curry is rich in flavours, it can simply be eaten with steamed rice and tomatoes and, Onion Sambal and Rassam

MEAT VARIATION

This recipe can be cooked with your favourite meats such as boned leg of lamb or pork loin or blade bone. Just use the same measurements and follow the recipe as per usual. The cooking time of these meats vary according to cuts of the meat. Remember to keep stirring throughout, check the tenderness of the meat when cooking and reduce the sauce to achieve a dry curry.

NB: If mutton (goat) is not available
lean lamb can be substituted.

Mutton Chops

INGREDIENTS

8 mutton chops OR lamb cutlets (ask your butcher for lean chops or cutlets)
1 medium firm tomato, finely chopped
1 medium Spanish onion, finely chopped
2 hot green chillies, de-seeded and finely chopped
1 small sprig fresh dill, finely chopped
2 eggs, lightly beaten
2 tablespoons tomato sauce
1 tablespoon Worcestershire sauce
2 teaspoons black pepper, coarsely cracked
Rock salt to taste
Breadcrumbs
Sunflower oil for frying

METHOD

With a sharp knife trim all fat off chops or cutlets.

Using a meat tenderiser, flatten mutton chop or cutlet, while keeping its original shape (flatten enough to fill with 1 tablespoon of filling) then set aside.

In a mixing bowl add onion, tomato, green chillies, cracked pepper and salt to taste.

Mix ingredients with the tomato, Worcestershire sauce and finely chopped dill and set aside.

On a baking tray, arrange flattened cutlets or chops.

Spoon a tablespoon of mixed ingredients and press firmly onto the meat of chops or cutlet and set aside.

Whisk eggs lightly in a shallow dish and set aside.

Place breadcrumbs on greaseproof paper and carefully dip each filled chop or cutlet into the egg and breadcrumbs until well coated. (Only one side of the chop or cutlets surface is filled with mixture.) (As a suggestion it is better to double coat the chops or cutlet in breadcrumbs.)

Once all chops or cutlets have been crumbed, wrap the bone of the chop or cutlet with foil (to avoid burning when frying).

Refrigerate for 1 hour until firm.

In a large frying pan, heat oil over a moderate heat and fry crumbed chops or cutlets until golden brown. (Be careful not to over fry as the lamb or mutton needs to be tender.) Drain on absorbent paper.

Serve hot.

In Sri Lanka this dish is often served as an accompaniment to a main meal. As a suggestion I would recommend this dish be served with steamed rice, Mutton Poriyal, Ash Plantain Curry and Prawn Varai. Mutton Chops are flavoursome, yet light, therefore it can be served as an entree with a dipping sauce of chilli mayonnaise.

TIP: Care must be taken when reusing the oil; remember to re-strain the oil while frying so that the oil is free of burnt breadcrumbs.
NB: If mutton (goat) is not available lean lamb can be substituted.

Kofta Curry ~ Goda Curry

Kofta Curry ~ Goda Curry

INGREDIENTS FOR KOFTA (SPICY MEATBALLS)

1 kg prime quality lamb mince
1 large white onion, finely sliced
2.5 cm piece ginger, ground
6 green chillies, finely chopped
1 teaspoon chilli powder
2 tablespoons Worcestershire sauce
1 tablespoon coarse black pepper
Salt to taste

INGREDIENTS FOR CURRY SAUCE

2 medium onions, finely diced
5 cloves garlic, finely chopped
2.5 cm piece of ginger, ground
1 sprig fresh curry leaves
1 teaspoon turmeric powder
1 tablespoon fennel seeds
1 tablespoon coriander seeds
1 teaspoon cumin seeds
4 cardamom pods
4 cloves
1 stick cinnamon
1 teaspoon black peppercorns
3 ripe tomatoes, finely diced
Juice of 1 fresh lime
2 cups coconut milk, diluted with equal parts
of water
3 tablespoons ghee
Salt to taste

METHOD FOR KOFTA

In a large mixing bowl, place mince, finely chopped onions, ginger and chillies.

Add chilli powder, Worcestershire sauce, pepper and salt to taste.

Using your hands, mix ingredients until well combined.

Wet hands and shape mixture into 5 cm balls and place on a tray.

Refrigerate until sauce is prepared.

METHOD FOR KOFTA CURRY SAUCE

In a heavy base pan over a medium heat, add fennel, coriander, cumin, black peppercorns, cinnamon, cardamoms, cloves and fresh curry leaves.

Dry-roast the spices for 3–4 minutes, while continuously shaking the pan or tossing the spices, so they don't scorch.

Allow to roast until spices are dark in colour and spice infused (as an indicator, the aroma of the coriander should smell sweet, cumin is nutty and curry leaves crispy).

Allow spices to cool.

Place cooled spices into a grinder and grind to a fine dark curry powder.

Heat ghee in a heavy base saucepan and fry onions until golden over a moderate heat.

Stir in ground ginger, garlic, tomatoes and cook very slowly over a low heat.

Pour in the coconut milk and stir continuously.

Add the kofta meatballs and simmer very gently for 20 minutes, stirring occasionally. Add lime juice and salt to taste.

Stir in the dark roasted curry powder and simmer for further 20 minutes or until meatballs have cooked and the sauce thickens. Serve hot.

This Kofta Curry is a Northern Sri Lankan variation and is best served with steamed rice and accompanied with Chilli Potatoes, Crispy Fried Fish and Onion Sambal.

Amma is a great cook, she tells me that most of her cooking and training came from her grandma who was a perfectionist when it came to cooking any type of food. Amma's Chicken Poriyal Curry is usually made with pieces of chicken on the bone. She says the inclusion of the bone makes it so much tastier! She used to wash the chicken so many times before cooking that I used to think it would disappear down the sinkhole!

She also always kept telling her Cooks that the smaller the pieces the tastier the curry and frankly I agree. I love sucking chicken bones until I've managed to suck out the entire flavour. She used to marinate the chicken pieces in turmeric, chilli powder and salt and set it aside while she prepared the fresh curry powder. The curry powder recipe was a 'hand-me-down' from her grandmother.

Amma takes after my Putti Aachie in many ways. When she prepares the ingredients, such as onion, garlic and ginger they are all so perfectly cut. She cooks the Poriyal in a wok. Firstly, she fries the fresh ingredients in ghee. Next she adds the chicken pieces and cooks it to seal in the flavours. Next she adds the coconut milk and simmers until the chicken is tender. When the chicken starts to simmer, she adds dark-roasted curry powder stirring through until the chicken is well-coated with spices and cooked until dry, finally adding some salt and lime juice to taste. She called it a Nai Poriyal, although some call it a Paal Poriyal.

The beautiful aromatic smells wafting out of the kitchen is just something I will never forget. My children and I would shout out "Aachie, when is lunch?", "Amma when is lunch, it does not take that long to finish off such an easy dish". Even though it took longer, and we were impatient, she would always say, "I like doing it the way I have been taught".

Aachie's Chicken Poriyal

Aachie's Chicken Poriyal

INGREDIENTS

1.25 kg chicken thighs
4 green chillies, finely chopped
1 Spanish onion OR white onion, finely chopped
4 cloves garlic, finely chopped
2.5 cm piece ginger, finely chopped
2.5 cm rampé (pandan leaf)
2.5 cm lemongrass, chopped finely
2 sprigs fresh curry leaves
2 tablespoons fennel seeds
1 tablespoon coriander seeds
1 teaspoon cumin seeds
1 teaspoon peppercorns
1 teaspoon turmeric powder
2 teaspoons hot chilli powder
2.5 cm stick cinnamon
4 cardamoms
4 cloves
2 cups coconut milk
3 tablespoons ghee
Lime juice to taste
Salt to taste

METHOD

Remove skin from the chicken and cut into 2.5 cm pieces.

Sprinkle chicken with salt, turmeric and chilli powder.

Place in a glass bowl and marinate for 1 hour in the refrigerator.

Dry-fry fennel, coriander, cumin, pepper seeds, cinnamon, cardamom and cloves over low heat until rich in colour, tossing from side.

Allow to cool, and then grind into a fine powder. Set aside.

Heat ghee or oil in a heavy base pan or wok and fry finely chopped onions until golden.

Add the chopped ginger, garlic, green chillies, rampé, thinly sliced lemongrass and fresh curry leaves and sauté over medium heat until aromatic.

Mix in marinated chicken pieces and cook to seal the flavours into the meat for about 5 minutes.

Add the coconut milk and stir and cook over medium heat for further 20 minutes, stirring from time to time until most of the liquid has evaporated.

Add the dark roasted curry powder through the chicken until it coats the meats.

Add lime juice and salt to taste.

Chicken Poriyal is a dry curry and therefore can be eaten with Pillau Rice, steamed rice, Roti Channai, and Thakkali Curry, White Potato Curry or Tomato and Onion Sambal.

I would always prepare very mild curries for my children when they were young as they were not accustomed to spicy food at such a young age. Sunny, Natasha and Johann called this dish 'Baby Chicken Curry' as youngsters. To this day, my daughters still ask me to make this dish for them, as well as for their children. Each time I prepare this dish for my children and grandchildren, I am taken back to the days of early motherhood where little feet and hands, wide-eyed faces and little giggles illuminated my kitchen...so precious ...so grateful!

Sunny & Tasha with their kids

Johann and his family

Baby Chicken Curry With Potatoes

INGREDIENTS

1.25 kg chicken thigh fillets, skinned and cut into
bite-size pieces
1 large onion, finely chopped
4 cloves garlic, finely chopped
1 teaspoon ginger, freshly chopped
1 sprig fresh curry leaves
1 teaspoon turmeric powder
2 tablespoons coriander powder
1 tablespoon fennel powder
1 tablespoon cumin powder
½ teaspoon fenugreek seed
4 large potatoes, peeled and cut into cubes
250 g ripe tomatoes, finely chopped
1 cup coconut milk
Juice of 1 lime
2 tablespoons Sunflower oil
Salt to taste

METHOD

Cut chicken into 2.5 cm pieces and marinate in turmeric and salt, place in a glass bowl and leave in a cool place while preparing the rest of the ingredients.

Heat oil in a deep frying pan or wok over high heat.

Add onions, and fry until golden, stir in the ginger, garlic, fenugreek seeds and fry until fragrant.

Add fresh curry leaves and when they begin to crackle, add the chopped tomatoes, and cook until almost soft.

Add the coriander, fennel, cumin powder and stir over medium to low heat, stirring and making sure that you don't burn the spices.

Stir-fry for 2 minutes until you can really smell the aroma.

Add the diced chicken and sauté for 5 minutes.

Add the cubed potatoes and salt to taste.

Pour in the coconut milk and bring to the boil.

Reduce heat and simmer for about 30 minutes stirring occasionally. (By now you should have a thick smooth sauce.)

Squeeze lime juice into sauce and add salt to taste.

This dish is splendid with Pillau, Pappadums and Mango Chutney.

Chettinad Chicken

Ramani, my special sister makes many exotically enticing dishes. On my last visit to Chennai, I was sitting in the kitchen having my chai (tea) while watching her make her version of Chettinad Chicken. When I tasted it I told her, "Ramani, the spices that you are preparing are almost similar to the Jaffna Chicken Poriyal". The many similarities and the distinctive tastes of both the dishes are so appetising.

Chettinad Chicken

INGREDIENTS

8 large chicken drumsticks
250 g Spanish onions OR white onions, finely chopped
3 cloves garlic, finely chopped
2.5 cm ginger, finely chopped
10–15 fresh green chilies, roughly chopped
1 bunch coriander leaves, finely chopped
2 sprigs fresh curry leaves
1 teaspoon turmeric powder
3 large ripe tomatoes, finely diced
2 teaspoons fennel seeds
1 teaspoon coriander seeds
½ teaspoon cumin seeds
2.5 cm cinnamon stick
4 cloves
4 cardamoms
1 teaspoon black peppercorns
2 tablespoons Sunflower oil
2 teaspoons salt

METHOD FOR SPICES

Marinate the chicken pieces in turmeric and salt, then set aside for half an hour.

Grind the ginger and garlic to a smooth paste.

In a heavy base frying pan, dry-roast fennel, coriander, cumin, peppercorn seeds and the remaining spices.

Tilt the pan from side to side, making sure that all spices are golden, and you can smell the different flavours, then allow it to cool.

Grind to form a powder and set aside.

METHOD FOR CHICKEN

Heat oil in a wok over a medium heat.

Add chopped green chillies and curry leaves, and fry until fragrant.

Add the chopped onions and cook until light golden brown in colour.

Add the tomatoes, ginger and garlic and cook until tomatoes are soft and the gravy forms into a smooth paste.

When the sauce begins to boil, add the marinated chicken pieces stirring over medium to low heat until well coated.

Add roasted spice mixture and salt, and slowly bring to the boil, reduce heat and gently simmer for 30 minutes or until the entire liquid gets absorbed and chicken is coated with spices.

Tandoori Chicken

Tandoori Chicken

INGREDIENTS

8 chicken breast fillets
2 teaspoons coriander powder
1 teaspoon cumin powder
2 teaspoons salt
Juice of 2 limes
12 dry chillies OR fresh hot chillies, ground to a fine paste
2 cups yoghurt, beaten until smooth and creamy
4 tablespoons ghee
1 teaspoon Garam Masala
4 teaspoons white vinegar
1 teaspoon orange food colouring (used for Tandoor foods and is available in Sri Lankan and Indian grocery stores)

METHOD

Clean and skin the chicken, then make a few slits on the breast.

Rub salt and lime juice on the chicken and set aside for 15 minutes.

Grind all dry ingredients and the ginger and garlic to a fine paste, add yoghurt and Tandoor colouring.

Add marinade and 2 tablespoons ghee to the chicken breast and refrigerate for 3 hours.

Cook in Tandoor (or if not available in a very hot oven at 425°C or under the grill for 15 minutes) and when chicken is almost cooked remove and baste it with ghee.

Return to oven cook for further 5 minutes.

Place on serving dish with a side dish of steamed rice, cucumber raita, lemon wedges and caramelised onion rings.

Tandoori Chicken is great served with Roti Channai, Tomato Curry or Chickpea and Potato Curry.
This dish is now ready to be served with steamed Basmati Rice, Chapatti or Roti Channai.

Chicken Palandi

Chicken Palandi

INGREDIENTS

1 kg chicken breast fillets
2 large Spanish onions, thinly sliced
4 cloves garlic, ground to a fine paste
2.5 cm piece fresh ginger, ground to a fine paste
6 green chillies, de-seeded and finely sliced
2 sprig fresh curry leaves
1 red capsicum OR green capsicum, thinly sliced
1 teaspoon chilli powder
1 teaspoon turmeric powder
1 teaspoon cracked pepper
250 g creamy natural yoghurt, whipped
3 tablespoons tomato paste
2 medium eggs, lightly beaten
2 teaspoons sugar
2 tablespoons Sunflower oil
2 tablespoons pure ghee
Salt to taste

METHOD

Brush chicken breast with olive oil then pan-fry in a wok for 3–4 minutes until cooked on both sides.

Set aside and slice into 3.5 cm thick strips.

Add ghee in a heavy base pan or wok over a medium-high heat, and then add ginger and garlic and sauté until aromatic.

Add fresh curry leaves, chilli and turmeric powder and cook until fragrant.

Add tomato paste and stir to form a smooth paste.

Reduce heat to low and add the sliced chicken, then continue to fold in the paste to coat the chicken pieces and fry for further 10 minutes.

Next add sliced onions, green chillies and capsicum and cook on a medium heat, while turning the chicken pieces.

Mix in whipped yoghurt and simmer over a low heat for 10 minutes.

Gently pour beaten eggs through the sauce, folding eggs slightly to scramble. (The sauce must have a lightly scrambled texture.)

Add salt and cracked pepper to taste.

This dish is a family favourite, especially when served with Yellow Rice or Roti Channai and Pappadums.

Kadai ~ Wok Style Chicken

Kadai ~ Wok Style Chicken

INGREDIENTS

1 kg mixed chicken pieces off the bone OR thigh
fillets, cut into 3.5 cm pieces
1½ cup tomatoes, finely chopped
½ cup Spanish onions OR white onions, finely
chopped
1 Spanish onion for garnishing cut into rings
1 tablespoon garlic, freshly ground
1 tablespoon ginger, freshly ground
4 hot red chillies, thinly sliced
½ tablespoon fresh coriander leaves, finely
chopped
2 bay leaves
1 teaspoon red chilli powder
1 teaspoon turmeric powder
3 teaspoons Garam Masala powder
2 teaspoons coriander seeds, coarsely ground
4 tablespoons Sunflower oil
Salt to taste

METHOD

Marinate chicken pieces in the chilli powder, turmeric powder and salt and set aside.

Grind coriander seeds and red chillies to a coarse paste (masala) in a grinder.

Heat oil in a Kaddai (a wok used for Indian cooking) over a medium heat.

Gradually add the onions and sauté until golden brown.

Add bay leaves, ginger and garlic and fry until aromatic for a further 2 minutes over a medium heat.

Add the coriander seeds and fresh red chilli masala (retain a little of the masala for later) and stir well.

Add the thinly sliced tomatoes and cook until soft and tender.

Cook over medium heat for a further 30 minutes and stir continuously.

Add the rest of the masala and cook until chicken is soft and tender.

Sprinkle the remaining masala and the Garam Masala over the chicken.

Garnish with finely chopped coriander leaves and onion rings.

Serve with Rice or South East Asian flat breads and Fried Fish Sambal.

Chicken Sarakku Curry

INGREDIENTS

1½ kg chicken thigh fillets
1 Spanish onion OR white onion, finely chopped
4 cloves garlic, finely chopped
3 cm piece ginger, finely chopped
4 green chillies, finely sliced
1 sprig curry leaves
3 tablespoons of Sarakku Thull curry powder
1 cup fresh scraped coconut OR desiccated coconut
2 cups warm water
Juice of 1 medium lime
2 tablespoons Sunflower oil
Salt to taste

METHOD

Cut chicken thigh fillets into 3.5 cm pieces and marinate in turmeric, Sarakku Thull and salt for 30 minutes.

Heat the oil in a pan and fry the onions until golden brown.

Add the chopped ginger and garlic and fry until fragrant.

Add fresh green chillies and fresh curry leaves and fry until transparent.

Add the marinated chicken fillets and fold through the fried mixture and cook for 10 minutes over medium heat.

Reduce heat and stir.

In a separate pan, dry-roast the coconut until golden, then allow it to cool.

Grind the coconut with a quarter cup of cold water to form a smooth paste.

Add this to the chicken, while adding the remaining water and simmer for another 30 minutes.

Add lime juice and salt to taste.

Serve with steamed White Rice, Dhal and Tomato and Onion Sambal.

226

Beef Badun

INGREDIENTS

1 kg stewing steak OR blade bone steak,
cut into 3 cm pieces
2 tablespoons coriander seeds
1 tablespoon fennel seeds
1 teaspoon cumin seeds
1 teaspoon fenugreek seeds
10 dry chillies
1 teaspoon turmeric powder
4 cloves garlic, finely chopped
5 cm piece fresh ginger, finely chopped
2 sprigs curry leaves
2 white onions, finely chopped
4 cm cinnamon stick
4 cardamoms, bruised
2.5 cm rampé (pandan), finely chopped
2.5 cm lemongrass, finely sliced
2 cups water
2 tablespoons ghee

METHOD

Dry-roast the spices until fragrant.

Allow to cool, and then grind in a spice grinder to
a fine powder.

Marinate meat with turmeric and salt.

Heat ghee in a large pan, add onions and fry
until golden.

Stir in fenugreek seeds, ginger, garlic, fresh curry
leaves, sliced lemongrass and rampé and cook until
fragrant.

Add the ground spice mix, stir through and cook until
it changes colour. (It should be dark brown in colour.)

Add marinated meat and stir through, making sure
meat is coated with spices.

Add cinnamon, cardamom, cloves and mix well.

Add water and cover with lid, then cook over a low
heat, stirring from time to time.

Simmer until meat is tender.

Add lemon juice and salt to taste and keep stir-frying
the meat until well coated with the spices and the
curry is almost dry.

Beef Smoore

INGREDIENTS

2½ kg topside OR sirloin beef, boned out
2 tablespoons chilli powder
2 tablespoons coriander seeds
1 tablespoon fennel seeds
1 teaspoon cumin seeds
1 teaspoon turmeric
2.5 cm cinnamon stick
2 sprigs fresh curry leaves
2.5 cm piece fresh root ginger, finely chopped
2.5 cm stalk lemongrass, finely chopped
2 tablespoons lime pickle, finely chopped
1 tablespoon white vinegar
1 tin coconut milk
2 cups water
4 tablespoons ghee
2 teaspoons salt

METHOD

Dry-roast spices until dark golden brown, stirring in a frying pan until fragrant.

Allow to cool.

Grind to a fine powder and set aside.

Add a little water.

Grind fresh curry leaves, pandan leaves, lemongrass, ginger and garlic to a fine paste.

Coat the meat in ground spices then add the paste and 2 tablespoons of ghee and mix and marinate for 2 hours.

Preheat oven to 180°C.

Heat ghee in large frying pan, add the meat and seal all sides until light brown in colour.

Remove from the frying pan and place in a baking dish.

Mix in the vinegar, coconut milk, finely chopped lime pickle and water.

Pour this into meat tray and cook for 1½ hours.

Slice meat and pour the pan juices over meat.

This dish is best served with Golden Yellow Rice, Thakkali Curry, White Potato Curry or Carrot and Onion Sambal.

Pepper Beef

Pepper Beef

INGREDIENTS

1 kg topside OR fillet of beef
2 large white onions OR Spanish onions, thinly sliced
250 g potatoes, peeled and cut into medium cubes
2 tablespoons Worcestershire sauce
2 tablespoon vinegar
2 tablespoons black peppercorns, coarsely ground
1 tablespoon dark roasted curry powder
2 tablespoons Sunflower oil
2 teaspoons salt

METHOD

Finely cut meat into 6 mm wide strips. (Freeze meat for 15 minutes before cutting—it becomes easier to cut into strips.)

Place in a deep bowl, marinate with Worcestershire sauce, coarse pepper and salt and set aside for 30 minutes.

Bring saucepan of water to the boil then add salt and cook potatoes until almost tender and drain.

Heat a large frying pan or wok, add oil and sauté beef fillets over a medium flame, and add vinegar and cook until almost dry.

Add the boiled potatoes, curry powder and onions, stir-fry until all ingredients are well blended.

Add salt to taste.

This dish is best served with Golden Yellow Rice, Thakkali Curry, White Potato Curry or Carrot and Onion Sambal.

Spicy Beef Curry

INGREDIENTS

1 kg blade steak OR stewing steak
2 tablespoons dark roasted curry powder
2 teaspoons chilli powder
1 large white onion, finely chopped
1 teaspoon turmeric powder
4 cloves garlic, finely chopped
2.5 cm fresh root of ginger, finely chopped
2 cm rampé (pandan), cut into small pieces
1 sprig fresh curry leaves
4 green chillies, thinly sliced
2 cm stalk lemongrass, thinly sliced
250 g ripe tomatoes, coarsely chopped
2 tablespoons tomato paste
1 tin coconut milk
2 tablespoon Sunflower oil
2 cups water
Add salt to taste

METHOD

Cut beef into 2.5 cm cubes and marinate in salt, turmeric, chilli powder and set aside for one hour.

Heat a medium-size heavy base saucepan, add oil and fry diced onions until golden.

Add ginger and garlic, then tomatoes and cook until sauce is thick and tomatoes are soft.

Add curry leaves, lemongrass and rampé and cook until ingredients are fragrant.

Reduce heat and add marinated meat, mixing well making sure the meat is coated with the spices.

Add water and simmer until meat is almost cooked.

Then add coconut milk and dark roasted curry powder.

Increase heat, add salt and cook until gravy is thick and meat is tender.

Desserts & Cakes

Chocolate Gateau

Chocolate Gateau

INGREDIENTS

250 g dark chocolate, broken into small pieces
250 g unsalted butter
1½ packet Marie OR Nice biscuits
250 g pure icing sugar
2 tablespoons cocoa powder, dissolved in ¼ cup warm water
2 teaspoons vanilla extract
4 large eggs
2 cups warm milk
24 cm round spring form pan (base measures 22 cm)

METHOD

Line the base and sides of the pan with baking paper, extending paper 2 cm above edge of pan.

Place chocolate on top of double boiler, or heat proof bowl over pan of simmering water and dissolve chocolate stirring occasionally until smooth. Allow to cool.

In a large mixing bowl, beat butter until creamy, next add icing sugar beating well until creamy.

Next add the melted chocolate and whip for few minutes while adding the yolks one at a time until well combined.

Fold stiffly beaten egg whites and vanilla extract into the chocolate cream mixture.

Spread a layer of the chocolate cream at the bottom of the baking pan.

Dip biscuits in warm milk and layer on top of the chocolate cream.

Repeat with alternate layers of cream and biscuits, making sure you have some chocolate cream left for decorating the top layer.

Freeze for 4 hours.

Turn the gateau over, on to a serving platter, decorate with remaining cream and dust cocoa powder and sprinkle chopped cashew nuts.

NB: You can make this in a round cake tin following the same method. Instead of having a traditional birthday cake why not enjoy your birthday celebration with a Chocolate Gateau instead? When frozen, it cuts beautifully into slices.

My grandchildren Sofia, Natai, Tyson & Denzel

My grandchildren Sofia & Stella

As a teenager I enjoyed making yummy mouth-watering desserts. Making desserts was a favourite hobby of mine, even before I tried my hands at curries. Some of my favourites are the chocolate and mango mousse, Kulfi and Gulab Jamuns.

When I ran my restaurant in Melbourne, the desserts mentioned above were on my menu and many people would enjoy them. There are different variations to these desserts in Sri Lanka but I would like to share my recipes with you. I treasure making these desserts particularly the Chocolate Gâteau and Chocolate Mousse, as my children and grandchildren absolutely adore them! From the tender age of two, my grandson, Denzel, lovingly gained an appreciation of his Grandma's Chocolate Mousse and Chocolate Gâteau. Ten years later, he has now become the family's connoisseur of these two desserts. While growing up, Denzel watched his Mum, Aunt Tashi and Uncle Johann enjoy these desserts. Although a fussy eater, the moment he tried these desserts we were assured of an empty dessert plate and a polite asking for seconds every time. Denzel was just blown away by these decadent desserts and would always ask me to make them on his visits to Sydney. He would say, "Garmos, I want you to make the Chocolate Gâteau (or Chocolate Biscuit Pudding as the Sri Lankans call it) or Chocolate Mousse". Not only Chocolate Gâteau and Chocolate Mousse have became a signature dessert in my family, but these desserts have a special place in my grandson's heart, where he would remember these special treats upon visiting Grandma's house.

Chocolate Mousse

Chocolate Mousse

INGREDIENTS

200 g dark chocolate, broken into
small pieces
4 eggs, separated
4 tablespoons unsalted butter
4 tablespoons caster sugar
2 teaspoons gelatine, dissolved in ¼
cup of hot water
300 ml thickened cream
1 teaspoon vanilla extract OR 2 tablespoons Grand Marnier liqueur
Double cream
Dark chocolate for decorating
Berries of your choice

METHOD

Place chocolate on top of a double boiler, or heat-proof bowl over pan of simmering water. (Do not allow water to touch base of bowl.)

Stir chocolate occasionally until smooth and set aside.

In a separate bowl beat egg whites until they form peaks.

Beat the egg yolk with an electric beater until pale and thick, adding sugar and butter gradually.

Add spoonfuls of melted chocolate using a spatula into egg yolk mixture, add essences to gelatine mixture, fold it alternatively with the thickened cream, and lastly fold in whites until well blended.

Pour mixture into pretty glasses, or set in a large bowl.

Refrigerate for at least 4 hours or overnight.

Serve with whipped cream, fresh berries and shaved chocolate.

NB: Plate the mousse by spooning it onto large white plates and drizzle with berry coulis, double cream and chocolate curls.

Gulab Jamuns

INGREDIENTS (SUGAR SYRUP)

1 kg caster sugar
10 cups water
10 bruised cardamom pods
1 teaspoon saffron strands
2 teaspoons rose essence
1 teaspoon yellow food colouring

INGREDIENTS (GULAB JAMUNS)

1 kg full cream powder milk
200 g semolina
150 g plain flour
250 g melted butter
800 ml full cream milk
1 teaspoon baking powder
1 teaspoon bicarbonate of soda
Oil for frying

METHOD FOR SUGAR SYRUP

Bring the water and sugar to the boil in a large heavy base saucepan and cook until sugar has dissolved.

Add cardamom pods, saffron strands, rose essence and yellow food colouring to give it a vibrant colour.

Allow to cool.

METHOD FOR GULAB JAMUNS

Place all dry ingredients in a large mixing bowl.

Add butter and milk, a little at a time, kneading well to make a soft dough.

On a board, roll dough into a sausage shape and divide into 5 cm balls in the palm of your hand.

Arrange them on a dish, cover with a damp cloth while you prepare to fry gulab jamuns.

Heat oil in a wok until hot, and then reduce heat to medium.

Add a few jamuns at a time, turn heat to low and fry evenly, stirring until golden.

When cooked they will pop up.

Pat dry on absorbent paper.

Add these to the syrup and let them soak in the syrup for at least 4 hours.

Serve with vanilla ice cream.

NB: Prepare sugar syrup before you begin to make the Gulab Jamuns so that you can immerse the fruits in syrup as soon they cool down.

NB: This dessert is best eaten within a week as the sugar syrup does not stay fresh for long. You can make a smaller quantity if preferred.

Date Cake

Date Cake

INGREDIENTS

250 g caster sugar
250 g plain flour
250 g seedless dates
1 cup water
250 g unsalted butter
2 teaspoons bicarbonate of soda
3 eggs
1 teaspoon vanilla extract

INGREDIENTS (BUTTER ICING)

500 g icing sugar
2 egg whites
125 g butter
1 teaspoon vanilla extract
½ teaspoon rose essence

METHOD

Cut dates into small pieces and place in a glass bowl.

Stir in the bicarbonate of soda and the water, stir through, cover and soak overnight.

Pre-heat oven to 350°F (180°C).

Grease a 24 cm round rectangular tin and line the bottom and sides with baking paper.

Beat butter and sugar until light and fluffy, then add eggs one at a time, beating well after each addition.

Sift flour over the creamy mixture and combine.

Using a wooden spoon, fold in the dates and vanilla essence until well combined.

Spread evenly in the tin and bake for 1 hour or until cooked.

Remove from oven and leave to cool in the tin for 6–8 minutes before turning on to a wire rack to cool.

METHOD FOR BUTTER ICING

Using an electric mixer, cream butter.

Add icing sugar and beat until smooth.

Add the lightly beaten egg whites a little at a time.

Add the vanilla and rose essence to form a smooth consistency.

Carefully spoon mixture onto the cake, and smooth over with a broad knife or spatula and allow icing to set before cutting.

Rose Flavoured Milk Puddings

Rose Flavoured Milk Puddings

INGREDIENTS (PUDDINGS)

1 cup milk
1 cup pouring cream
2 teaspoons gelatine
⅓ cup caster sugar
1 teaspoon rose essence
4 tablespoons cold water

INGREDIENTS (ROSE SYRUP)

2 cups water
½ cup caster sugar
1 teaspoon lemon rind, finely grated
2 teaspoons rose essence

METHOD FOR PUDDINGS

Dissolve gelatine in the water in a pan and allow to soak, stirring until smooth.

Meanwhile, pour cream and milk into a heavy base saucepan, and cook over low heat, constantly stirring.

Bring ingredients to almost boiling point and then add gelatine and stir until it softens.

Remove from heat, allow it to cool, and then add rose essence.

Pour mixture through a sieve into a separate jug.

Spoon mixtures into 8 small moulds and refrigerate to set for approximately 3–4 hours.

To release the milk puddings from the moulds, dip each mould in a container of warm water and run a knife around the edge. Place on serving plates.

METHOD FOR ROSE SYRUP

Bring the sugar and water to the boil in a medium pan and cook over medium heat until syrupy.

Add rose essence and zest of lemon and cook for further 5 minutes.

Drizzle rose syrup over the puddings.

NB: These puddings are great with edible rose petals to garnish or with tangy fruits to complement sweetness and richness of this dessert. Alternatively you can serve it with a tangy passion fruit or mango coulis.

Orange Cake

Amma's Traditional Orange Cake

INGREDIENTS

Eggs
250 g plain flour, sifted
10 g corn flour
2 teaspoons baking powder
250 g unsalted butter, softened
250 g caster sugar
¼ cup orange juice, freshly squeezed and strained 1 teaspoon orange essence

INGREDIENTS (ORANGE CURD)

2 oranges, freshly squeezed and strained
2 medium eggs, well beaten
175 g caster sugar
60 g unsalted butter, softened and cut into chunks

INGREDIENTS (SNOW GLAZE)

1¼ cup icing sugar
1 teaspoon butter, softened
¼ teaspoon vanilla essence
4–6 teaspoons milk
3 tablespoons golden syrup
2 oranges for decoration

METHOD FOR CAKE

Pre-heat the oven to 180°C (355°F).

Place the softened butter in a large mixing bowl and beat till creamy.

Add sugar and beat until light and fluffy.

Add one egg at a time, beating well after each addition until well combined.

Gradually fold in strained orange juice and vanilla essence.

Fold in sifted flour and baking soda.

Spoon cake mixture evenly into a lightly greased 22 cm round tin, lined with non-stick baking paper.

Bake for 40 minutes.

Remove from oven and let the cake stand for 5 minutes before turning it on to a cake rack to cool.

Once cooled slice the cake into 2 layers and set aside.

METHOD FOR ORANGE CUSTARD

Grate zest of oranges and set aside.

Squeeze juice of 2 oranges, place in a glass bowl and add grated orange zest.

Beat eggs and half the sugar until thick and glossy in an electric beater

Place the glass bowl over a pan of boiling water and add butter and remaining sugar, the egg mixture and stir until well mixed.

Cook for 20 minutes, stirring frequently, until the mixture is a thick custard.

Remove from heat and allow the custard to cool.

ASSEMBLING CAKE WITH ORANGE CUSTARD

Pour the orange custard over one layer of cake and spread evenly. Reassemble to form 1 whole cake.

Transfer cake onto a serving platter.

METHOD FOR SNOW GLAZE

Combine icing sugar, butter, vanilla and milk.

Heat in a double saucepan with boiling water and stir until blended.

Spread evenly over the cake using a spatula.

Finally drizzle with golden syrup, and finely shredded zest of two oranges.

Sri Lankan Christmas Cake

INGREDIENTS

500 g unsalted butter
500 g caster sugar
125 g plain flour
500 g semolina
24 yolks
8 egg whites
500 g sultanas
250 g candid peel
1½ jars strawberry jam
500 g pumpkin preserve
250 g ginger preserve
250 g raisins
250 g raw cashew nuts
250 g glace cherries
250 g chow chow
(available in Asian supermarkets)
1 bottle brandy essence
1 bottle raspberry essence
1 bottle almond essence
2 oz brandy
6 heaped teaspoons mixed spices

INGREDIENTS (ALMOND PASTE TOPPING)

8 cups icing sugar
4 cups ground almonds OR
almond meal
6 egg whites
4 teaspoons rose essence
4 teaspoons sweet sherry
4 teaspoons lemon juice
16 tablespoons icing sugar (extra)

INGREDIENTS (JAM TOPPING)

1 cup water
½ cup strawberry jam
2 tablespoons white sugar

METHOD FOR CAKE

Combine all fruits, chopped nuts and jam in a food processor.

Slowly process, using the pause button so that you don't make a pulp of it.

Place in a large glass bowl, mix in the plain flour and leave aside to marinate.

Set aside and leave overnight or for 48 hours.

The next day:

In a heavy base saucepan lightly roast semolina and allow it to cool.

Add a tablespoon of butter, stir through and add to the fruit mixture.

Fold to combine.

Line two 30 cm x 22 cm deep sided oblong cake pans.

Brush with cooking oil, then line the base with 3 layers grease proof paper.

Pre-heat the oven to 150°C (350°F).

Cream the butter and caster sugar until light and fluffy.

Add egg yolks one at a time beating well after each addition.

Fold in semolina with the mixed spices, essences, brandy and spoon in the fruit mixture, folding through until combined.

Lastly fold in the stiffly beaten egg whites.

Spoon cake mixture into the tins evenly and bake for 2 hours.

Do not over bake cake.

METHOD FOR ALMOND PASTE TOPPING

Sift sugar into a bowl and add ground almonds.

Mix and make a well in the middle.

Beat the egg whites, sweet sherry and lemon juice together.

Pour into sugar and almond mixture and gradually work into a smooth paste, kneading well with both hands.

Lightly sprinkle some icing sugar on a workbench and roll out dough to fit the cakes, making dough 5mm thick.

METHOD FOR JAM TOPPING

Spread the jam topping still warm over the cake and roll the almond paste to fit cake.

NB: Make cake 2 months before Christmas, and pour cognac on top of cake once a week until Christmas. Store in an airtight tin until required.

Amma's Traditional Love Cake

INGREDIENTS

250 g semolina, coarse
500 g raw cashew nuts, finely chopped
500 g pumpkin preserve finely chopped
500 g caster sugar
250 g unsalted butter
12 egg yolks
4 egg whites, stiffly beaten to form peaks
½ bottle rose essence
1 wine glass pure bees honey
1 wine glass brandy
1 teaspoon mixed spices
Rind of 2 lemons, finely shredded

Meringue crust:

2 egg whites
½ cup caster sugar
Beat egg whites with an electric beater
until stiff, then add caster sugar gradually
and beat until glossy. Spread this mixture
evenly over the cake mixture and bake to
give a hint of a crunchy cake texture.

METHOD

Pre-heat oven to 150°C (300°F).

Lightly grease a rectangular cake tin (33 cm x 22 cm) with four
layers greased proof paper, to cover the sides and the bottom.

Roast semolina until golden and allow it to cool.

Beat in butter and set aside.

Beat with an electric beater the egg yolks in a large mixing
bowl until light and pale in colour, then gradually add the
caster sugar and beat well until air bubbles form.

Fold in the finely chopped cashew nuts, pumpkin preserve,
spices and the essences.

Using a wooden spoon, fold the lemon rind and beat in the
semolina mixture until thoroughly combined.

Fold in the stiffly beaten egg whites and bake for approximately 1 hour.

Turn oven off and leave to stand for 5 minutes before taking
the cake out of the oven.

Allow to cool, and then turn over onto a wire rack, leaving
paper on the cake.

Wrap cake in clean greaseproof paper and store cake in a cool
place until ready to use.

Amma's Chocolate Layered Cake

Amma's Chocolate Layered Cake

INGREDIENTS

220 g sifted self-raising flour
220 g caster sugar
180 g softened margarine
3 eggs
125 g softened unsalted butter
250 g dark chocolate
2 cups thickened cream
1½ tablespoons of cocoa powder,
dissolved in 3 tablespoons boiling water
1 teaspoon orange essence

METHOD

Pre-heat your oven to 160°C (320°F).

Grease and line a 22 cm round cake tin with 2 sheets of non-stick baking paper.

Place margarine and sugar in a deep mixing bowl and beat with an electric mixer on a medium speed until light and creamy.

Gradually add one egg at a time, beating well after each addition.

Fold in the cocoa that has been dissolved in the boiling water and beat well.

Fold in the flour until well combined.

Spoon mixture into the greased lined cake tin and bake in oven for 35–40 minutes or until cooked.

Remove from oven and let cake stand for 5 minutes.

Turn cake out onto cake rack.

Pour thickened cream into mixing bowl and whip until thick and creamy.

Refrigerate, while preparing chocolate filling.

Break up chocolate and place in a heatproof bowl.

Fill a medium-size saucepan with hot water (be careful not to overfill the saucepan).

Place bowl filled with chocolate over hot water and place over a medium heat.

Allow chocolate to melt to a creamy consistency, then remove and set aside to cool slightly.

In the meantime whip butter to a smooth, light and creamy texture then gradually add the melted chocolate.

Fold in the orange essence, and mix until well combined to form a smooth texture.

Once the cake has cooled, use a long sharp knife and split the cake in half and fill with whipped cream mixture.

Replace top, spread chocolate cream mixture over cake and top with remaining cream, chocolate swirls or little rosettes with the use of an icing bag.

Bibinca

Bibinca

INGREDIENTS

1 kg white sugar
16 egg yolks
2 cups plain flour
2 teaspoons nutmeg, grated
500 g thick coconut milk
250 g pure ghee

METHOD

Pre-heat the oven to 150°C (300°F).

Beat egg yolk and sugar in a bowl using an electric mixer, until thick and pale.

Using a whisk, gently fold in coconut milk and nutmeg.

Gradually fold in the flour until all ingredients are well combined.

Melt ghee and generously brush a 24 cm round cake with ghee.

Pour 2 cups of mixture into cake tin and bake for 20 minutes.

When layer is ready, brush top layer of cake with some ghee, pour two cups of mix and bake for another 20 minutes or until a skewer is inserted in the middle comes out clean.

Continue with the same process until you are left with the last 2 cups.

Brush the last layer with ghee and bake in a moderate oven until top layer is like a sponge to touch.

Allow to cool in the oven.

The next day:

Immerse cake tin in hot water as it makes it easy to turn it out on to a platter.

Pineapple Upside Down Cake

Pineapple Upside Down Cake

INGREDIENTS (CAKE)

1½ cup plain flour
2 teaspoons baking soda
125 g unsalted butter
1 cup caster sugar
4 eggs
1 teaspoon vanilla essence

INGREDIENTS (TOPPING)

75 g unsalted butter
250 g coconut palm sugar or jaggery
(available at Asian supermarkets)
½ cup water
1 tin pineapple rings

METHOD

Pre-heat oven to 180°C (355°F).

Place water in a medium-size saucepan.

Chop coconut and palm sugar roughly, add to water and place on medium heat.

Allow to dissolve and thicken while stirring.

Once thickened reduce heat and set aside.

Use a 20 cm round cake tin and grease it generously.

Arrange the pineapple rings in a circle and 1 ring in the centre of tin.

Pour the coconut palm sugar syrup from the centre to evenly spread at the bottom of the cake tin.

Sieve flour and baking powder together.

Use an electric mixer to cream butter until light.

Gradually add sugar and beat until thick and creamy.

Add eggs one at a time, beating well after each addition.

Lastly, gently fold in the sifted flour and baking powder into the creamy mixture.

Pour cake mixture over pineapple rings and syrup and bake in 180°C oven for 1 hour, or until cooked. (Test with a skewer.)

The cake should be golden in colour.

Once ready, allow cake to cool in the cake tin for 5 minutes.

To turn the cake, use a thin knife slide around edges of cake tin.

Place on a glass platter.

Use the remaind syrup to drizzle over the cake.

After I sold the restaurant, I moved to Sri Lanka for few years, and while I was there I had the opportunity to work for a large Sri Lankan/Chinese collaboration restaurant that served Peking and Szechwan food. I had learnt many new dishes, and on my days off as I did private catering, making desserts like Crème Caramel with Poached Pears, Passion Fruit Cheesecake, Pavlova with Passion Fruit Topping. Sri Lanka has beautiful fresh passion fruits. These desserts were carried with me from Australia to Sri Lanka. Friends and family would often ask me to make these delightful desserts at their dinner parties back in the early 1980s. What a joy it was to prepare these desserts after enjoying an elaborate meal of Sri Lankan rice and curry. The delicate tangy and citrus flavours of the Passion Fruit Cheesecake are a great way to end a traditional Sri Lankan meal.

When I used to make Crème Caramel for friends or families in Sri Lanka, it brought back memories of my restaurant days in Melbourne. I used to make Crème Caramel in the 70s at the restaurant, and the kids loved it. It was their all time favourite dessert. What I liked about this dessert was how easy it was to prepare and how much fun I had decorating it. I have always loved making it just to see their gleaming faces. It was also a popular dessert at formal or funky dinner parties along with flared pants, disco fashion and Saturday Night fever during the 1970s. Whatever the occasion, the plates always came back empty. As an accompaniment, I liked to serve it with poached pears, which not only fuses this smooth crème, but also looks pleasing. Adding thickened cream through a piping bag re-creates the retro appeal of the 70s and also gives the palate an array of textured flavours.

Crème Caramel

256

Crème Caramel With Poached Pears

INGREDIENTS (CRÈME CARAMEL)

4 cups full cream milk
1 vanilla bean OR 1 teaspoon vanilla
extract
350 g sugar
6 eggs

INGREDIENTS (CARAMEL SAUCE)

200 g caster sugar
¼ cup cold water

INGREDIENTS (POACHED PEARS)

4 small medium half ripe pears, peeled
(attempt to leave stalks on each fruit
while stewing)
160 g caster sugar
1 small lemon, peeled
2 cups water
1 cinnamon stick
300 ml thickened cream for decorating

NB: This dessert is best served when prepared
the night before

NB: Using your creativity, come up with a
design of your own. I hope that you enjoy this
irresistible dessert with your loved ones, family and friends as much as I do! Poached Pears
is such a versatile accompaniment. It can be
served on its own or served with Vanilla Bean
Sorbet or Crème Anglaise.

METHOD FOR CARAMEL SAUCE

Place the sugar and water into a medium-size heavy base saucepan and place over a medium heat until dissolved, then bring to the boil and simmer until mixture becomes a caramel colour.

Remove from heat and pour evenly into a 22 cm round cake or into 8 round ramekin dishes tipping it for even contribution.

Leave aside and begin to make the crème.

METHOD FOR CRÈME DE LA CRÈME

Preheat oven to 160°C (325°F).

Pour milk into a medium-size heavy base saucepan, add vanilla bean or vanilla extract, then place over a medium heat until near boiling point, and remove from heat.

Whisk eggs in a large ceramic bowl until stiff.

Add sugar, whisking until sugar is mixed well.

Strain warm boiled milk into egg mixture, stirring until custard is well blended.

Pour mixture into cake tin or ramekin dishes.

Place the cake tin or dishes in a deep baking dish filled with boiling water that reaches half way level at sides of tin or dishes and bake for 50–60 minutes in the middle section of the oven.

Once surface of caramel is golden in colour, remove from oven, allow to cool.

Refrigerate at least for 6 hours before serving.

When ready to serve, loosen sides of tin or ramekin dishes with a thin sharp edged knife.

Place a large serving dish over the top of the tin or individual serving plate over ramekin dish.

Firmly holding the plate and tin (or ramekin dish), turn the crème caramel onto the plate.

Now we begin the creative part of decorating retro style!

METHOD FOR POACHED PEARS

Poach pears with sugar, lemon peel, cinnamon stick and water in a medium-size saucepan until sugar has melted.

Taste and add more sugar if necessary.

Drop pears and simmer for 10–15 minutes.

Let the pears cool in the syrup and then slice the pears in halves or quarters.

Keep remaining syrup for serving.

(As a preference I like to leave the pear stems on for a rustic look however, you can remove them for a more finished look.)

Set aside on a plate until you are ready to decorate your crème caramel.

In the meantime, whip your pouring or thickened cream until it forms peaks, refrigerate.

Kulfi Ice Cream

Kulfi Ice Cream

INGREDIENTS

1 litre full cream milk
2 cups pouring cream
125 g cashew OR almond meal, ground
395 g tin condensed milk
4 tablespoons cornflour
1 teaspoon rose essence
⅔ cup caster sugar
3 cardamom pods, finely bruised

METHOD

In a mixing bowl, whisk together milk, cream and corn flour until well blended.

Place mixture into a medium heavy base saucepan over medium heat.

Bring the mixture to boiling point, then reduce heat and whisk constantly until smooth.

Add the condensed milk, sugar, ground cashew (or almond) meal, rose essence and cardamom pods.

Mix ingredients while simmering until all ingredients are well combined and a creamy consistency is obtained and then allow it to cool.

Pour the creamy mixture into the Kulfi cones or moulds.

Wrap or cover the cones or moulds carefully, making sure no air gets into it, while you freeze the ice cream for 6–8 hours or overnight.

NB: You will need 8 metal Kulfi moulds available in Indian grocery store or 8 x ½ cup capacity moulds.
NB: For variety you can flavour Kulfi ice cream with crushed pistachios and green food colouring, Spanish Saffron and yellow food colouring, vanilla bean and almond flakes and pink food colouring with rose essence.

Mango Mousse

Mango Mousse

INGREDIENTS

4 ripe sweet mangoes OR 500 g
mango pulp
Alfonzo (available from Indian spice
shops)
2 cups thickened cream
¾ cup caster sugar
Juice of 1 lemon
1 tablespoon gelatine
½ cup cold water

METHOD FOR MOUSSE

Peel mango, cut away from the seeds and blend to a pulp.

Add caster sugar, lemon juice and blend until all ingredients are mixed well, and then set aside.

Sprinkle gelatine over the water and stand in a pan of simmering water or dissolve in the microwave for 20 seconds. Allow to cool.

Beat cream in a large mixing bowl with an electric mixer until thick.

Fold in the mango mixture and gelatine into cream mixture.

Spoon the mixture into individual flute glasses or pour into 8 x ½ cup moulds and refrigerate until set.

The mousse can be garnished with thinly sliced mangos or drizzle with dark melted chocolate.

TIP: When using the moulds immerse them in lukewarm water for about 20 seconds and turn on to a serving plate.

Palm Sugar Sago Pudding

Palm Sugar Sago Pudding

INGREDIENTS

½ cup pure palm sugar OR jaggery
½ cup caster sugar
¼ cup water (to dissolve palm sugar)
2 cups sago OR tapioca
Pinch of salt
500 ml water
2 cups coconut milk
Extra ½ cup creamy coconut milk for serving

METHOD

Pre-soak sago in cold water for a few hours and rinse until water is clear.

If using a block of palm sugar or jaggery, chop it roughly into chunks or alternatively you can grate it and set aside.

Place palm sugar in a heavy base medium pan with a ¼ cup of water and bring to the boil until palm sugar is dissolved.

Gently stir until a fairly thick consistency is formed.

Once caramelised, pour into moulds and set aside at room temperature.

Place water, sugar, coconut milk, salt and the drained sago into a medium-size frying pan and cook over a low heat stirring, constantly until sago has swelled. (Do not allow mixture to boil.)

Gently pour sago mixture into caramel-lined moulds and refrigerate for 6 hours or until set.

When serving, dip moulds in hot water to loosen caramel and turn onto 8 serving plates. (It can be helpful to gently scrape a butter knife along the edges of the moulds.)

Pour remaining palm sugar caramel and drizzle with creamy coconut milk.

Panipol Pancakes

Panipol Pancakes

INGREDIENTS (PANCAKES)

1 cup plain flour
2 eggs
1½ cups coconut milk
A pinch of salt

INGREDIENTS (COCONUT FILLING)

250 g pure palm sugar
250 g shredded coconut OR desiccated coconut
¾ cup water
1 teaspoon vanilla essence

METHOD FOR PANCAKES

Make a light pancake batter by combining coconut milk and beaten eggs and gradually fold in the flour.

Stir until ingredients are well combined and beat until smooth.

Pour 2 tablespoons of batter into a greased non-stick 20 cm frying pan (to make thin pancakes).

Allow pancakes to cool.

METHOD FOR COCONUT FILLING

Place palm sugar and water in a large saucepan and cook over medium heat, stirring constantly.

Add grated coconut and cook until coconut is well coated with palm sugar.

Add vanilla essence and allow mixture to cook until fairly thick, and then cool.

Place pancakes on flat surface, fill with coconut mixture and wrap into small packages.

This dessert can be served hot or cold. The pancakes are exotically flavoured, especially when infused with vanilla bean ice cream and treacle on the side.

Palm Sugar Baked Custard

Palm Sugar Baked Custard

INGREDIENTS

500 g pure palm sugar (Indonesian palm sugar)
400 ml coconut milk
375 g Carnation evaporated milk
10 large eggs
100 g cashew nuts, finely chopped
1 teaspoon nutmeg, grated
1 teaspoon cardamom powder
2 teaspoons vanilla essence
250 ml water

METHOD

Pre-heat the oven to 180°C (350°F).

Coarsely chop the palm sugar and place in a large saucepan.

Add the water and cook over a medium heat until sugar is dissolved and the syrup is thick, allow it to cool.

Meanwhile, beat eggs until thick and creamy, add the coconut milk, evaporated milk, spices and vanilla essence and mix well together.

Finally fold in the palm sugar mixture.

Pour mixture into 8 x 1 cup capacity greased individual pudding dishes.

Place them in an oblong cake tin with enough boiling water to cover the bottom half of the dishes, then bake for 1 hour or until set.

Remove from oven and allow to cool for about 8 hours.

When ready to serve, run a knife around the edge and turn out the desserts onto serving plates.

Drizzle with melted palm sugar syrup and finely chopped cashew nuts.

This custard is easy to make and requires no preparation time, but importantly it has to be eaten within 48 hours.

This custard must be chilled well prior to serving, to bring out the flavour and consistency.

Passion Fruit Cheesecake

INGREDIENTS

250 g Philadelphia cream cheese
395 g condensed milk
300 ml thickened cream
3 teaspoons gelatine
Juice of 1 lemon
Rind of 1 lemon, finely shaved
1 packet Marie OR Nice Biscuits
150g unsalted butter
¼ cup water

INGREDIENTS (PASSION FRUIT TOPPING)

10 ripe fresh passion fruits
1 small tin concentrated passion fruit
pulp (with the seeds to garnish)
2 cups water
½ cup caster sugar
2 teaspoons gelatine
3 tablespoons corn flour
3 tablespoons caster sugar

METHOD FOR BISCUIT BASE

Grease a 24 cm round spring foam pan (base measure 22cm) and line sides with baking paper, extending 2 cm above the edge of pan.

To make the biscuit base, process biscuits in a food processor and blend until crushed and finely chopped, or place in a plastic bag and run a rolling pin over until crushed, then set aside.

Melt butter in a small saucepan over a medium heat and pour over the biscuits, stirring until well combined.

Press biscuit mixture over base of the prepared pan.

Refrigerate while preparing filling.

METHOD FOR CREAMY FILLING

Beat cream cheese, sugar, lemon rind and juice with an electric mixer until light and creamy.

Add condensed milk and continue to beat on low to medium speed, adding the gelatine (which has been dissolved).

Gently fold thickened cream into cream cheese mixture until ingredients are mixed through.

Spoon mixture into prepared pan, cover, refrigerate and allow it to set for 5 hours.

METHOD FOR CREAMY FILLING

Remove pulp from the passion fruits.

Combine all ingredients except passion fruit pulp in a medium-size pan.

Place over a low heat and stir until the topping is thick and has a smooth consistency.

Use your spoon as an indicator; if it forms a thick coat on the back of spoon and does not drip, it is the right texture.

Allow to cool for 15 minutes, then spread the passion fruit mixture over cheesecake and refrigerate until set.

Remove cheesecake from pan and place on a serving plate.

Serve with extra whipped cream if desired or just enjoy it the way it is.

Sticky Date Pudding With Creamy Custard

Sticky Date Pudding With Creamy Custard

INGREDIENTS (PUDDING)

170 g self-raising flour
170 g caster sugar
60 g unsalted butter
2 eggs, lightly beaten
50 g preserved ginger, finely chopped
170 g of pitted dates
½ teaspoon vanilla essence
1 teaspoon bicarbonate of soda
300 ml water

INGREDIENTS (CUSTARD)

250 ml full cream milk
250 ml single cream
5 egg yolks
75 g caster sugar
1 teaspoon vanilla extract

INGREDIENTS (CARAMEL SAUCE)

100 g unsalted butter
200 g brown sugar
½ cup thick cream
1 teaspoon vanilla essence

METHOD FOR PUDDING

Chop dates coarsely and place in medium-size saucepan.

Add water and bicarbonate soda.

Cook gently until dates are soft and the mixture is dark in colour.

Allow dates to cool and set aside.

Meanwhile, beat butter and sugar until fluffy.

Add one lightly beaten egg one at a time.

Fold in flour and lastly the cooled date mixture.

Add finely chopped preserved ginger and pour into individual buttered ramekin dishes, or into a well-buttered 24 cm round cake tin.

Bake at 160°F for 50 minutes or until cake has risen in the centre and soft to touch in the centre.

Allow puddings to cool and serve with warm custard or caramel sauce

METHOD FOR CUSTARD

Bring a pan of water to boil or alternatively use a double boiler on a hot stove.

Place cream, milk and eggs in a glass bowl and whisk until well blended.

Reduce heat to medium, set the bowl over the boiling water and add vanilla extract whisking continuously.

Reduce heat to very low, add sugar and continue to simmer for 3–4 minutes until custard begins to thicken.

Remove from heat and allow the custard to cool.

METHOD FOR CARAMEL SAUCE

Combine all ingredients in a pan over a low heat and stir constantly until you have a smooth sauce.

Spoon over the cooled cake and serve with a dollop of cream.

Payasam

Payasam is a traditional South Indian dessert. It is very similar to a rice pudding but lighter in consistency. This creamy sweet pudding is quick and easy to make. There are many versions and I have chosen to share a few that I grew up with. As I mentioned earlier, I grew up in my grandparents' home at St Edwin's. I was born into a Hindu family and therefore the family followed Hindu religious beliefs and traditions. On Fridays, Kandiah used to make Payasam for dessert and we would enjoy this on a weekly basis. Kandiah, who was the cook at my grandparents' home, always made the Coconut Milk and Sago version. It had a hint of rose flavour, cashew nuts and sultanas, and it was scrumptious. Tamils make this dessert to celebrate New Year's Day and Hindu weddings. It is also eaten on auspicious days, and on days when vegetarian food is prepared.

INGREDIENTS

200 g sago OR tapioca
1 litre milk
3 cups water
6 tablespoon ghee
100 g cashew nuts, coarsely chopped
100 g sultanas
6 cardamom pods, bruised
100 g caster sugar
100 g semiya (similar to vermicelli)
1 teaspoon rose essence

PREPARATION

Soak sago for one hour in cold water rinse until water is clear.

Add water, milk and sugar and pour into a heavy base saucepan, and bring to the boil, stirring until tapioca seeds have dissolved to produce a fairly smooth thick liquid. Set aside.

In separate frying pan, heat ghee until hot, then add cashew nuts and roast until golden over a medium heat and set aside.

Next add sultanas and semiya and toss gently until light golden in colour.

Add these fried ingredients into sago and stir well. Now add the cardamom and rose essence simmer for five minutes.

Payasam can be served hot or cold. It is a beautiful dessert that complements vegetarian dinner menus.

Pongal

Pongal is a sweet rice dish made of jaggery, cashew nuts, fresh sultanas, coconut milk and cardamom. This is normally made on Thai Pongal, which takes place during the second week in January. 'Thai' in Tamil means the month of 'January'. The celebration is a thanks giving to nature and the Sun which has provided a successful harvest.

Pongal ~ Sticky Rice

INGREDIENTS

250 g white sticky rice OR country rice
2 cups water
200 g jaggery OR palm sugar
⅔ cup fresh milk OR Canned coconut milk
½ cup raw cashew nuts, coarsely chopped
2 tablespoons clarified butter (ghee)
1 teaspoon mixed spices (cardamom,
cloves and cinnamon)
½ teaspoon rose essence
½ teaspoon salt
2 banana leaves

METHOD

Soak rice in a bowl of cold water for 2 hours.

Drain and cook rice with water as normal.

In a separate pan gently stir together palm sugar and coconut milk
or fresh milk, until sugar is dissolved.

Add this mixture to the rice and cook stirring on low heat until rice
is soft, fold in sultanas, chopped nuts and rose essence.

Blanched banana leaf in boiling water for a few seconds and pat
dry with a paper towel.

Spread a layer of the sticky rice evenly pressing down with the
other leaf to make it even all around. Cut into diagonal shapes and
serve warm or cold.

N.B: This sweet rice dish tastes nice when served with a scoop of vanilla ice cream or with fresh mango or banana.

Pumpkin Preserve

Pumpkin Preserve

INGREDIENTS

500 g pumpkin (winter welon - fruit
found in many Asian markets)
500 g white sugar
1 cup water
1 teaspoon rose essence

METHOD

Peel the pumpkin, cut in half and remove seeds from inside the fruit. Divide pumpkin into sections and cut them into 1 inch squares. Set aside while you begin to prepare the syrup.

Put sugar and water into a preserving saucepan, bring to the boil, and keep stirring the syrup until it is a very thick.

Add the cut pieces of pumpkin after squeezing off any excessive water. Cook, stirring constantly and making sure the sugar does not stick to the pan.

Add the rose essence while the sugar syrup is thickening and reducing.

Reduce heat when the pumpkin crystallises, to a soft ball stage. Pour into a square dish and leave to set like soft fudge. Cut into diamond shapes and use as required.

In Sri Lanka pumpkin preserve is eaten like any other sweet after a meal.

INGREDIENTS

250 g semolina
100 g clarified butter
100 g cashew nuts, finely diced
3 cups water
1 litre milk
1 teaspoon saffron strands
½ teaspoon rose essence OR rose water
100 g sultanas
100 g white sugar
2 cardamom pods, bruised
Kernel of thambili (young coconut),
finely chopped

METHOD

Melt clarified butter in a pan stir fry cashew nuts until golden.

Remove from heat and leave aside to cool.

Gently toss in the sultanas until they change colour.

Drain the butter and save until you prepare the other ingredients.

In a large frying pan, dry-roast semolina until it changes colour. Set aside.

Bring the milk and water to boil and then simmer, adding sugar, saffron strands and bruised cardamoms.

Add the semolina, stirring gently on a very low heat.

Garnish with cashew nuts, sultanas, roasted semolina and coconut kernel.

Serve hot or cold.

Dinner Party Menus

Planning a dinner party? It may be someone's birthday or just a general celebration of glorious food! Either way, both are great excuses for having a lunch or a dinner party for friends or your loved ones. I've put together a few suggested menus, featuring great finger food recipes and a choice of vegetarian, seafood and meat dishes, rice and desserts.

Menu 1

Potato Bonda	Raal Appam
Mutton Chops	Golden Yellow Rice
Chicken Palandy	Turmeric Crust Egg Curry
Fried Fish Curry	Brinjal Pahi
Dhal Curry	Mixed Vegetable Pickle
Mint Chutney	Mango Mousse
Ravai Payasm	

Menu 2

Vegetable Pancake Rolls	Mutton Chops
Lamb Biriyani	Fluffy White Rice
Chicken Poriyal	Beef And Potato Curry
Pineapple Curry	Brinjal Pahi
Mint Chutney	Chilli Potatoes
Tomato And Onion Sambal	Eggplant And Onion Salad
Palm Sugar Crème Brulee	Pistachio Kulfi

Menu 3

Vegetarian Pan Rolls	Tandoori Chicken Drumsticks
Vegetable Pillau	Lamb Korma
Fish Moilee	Blackened Pork Curry
Tomato Curry	Vegetable Kofta Curry
Mixed Vegetable Pickle	Carrot And Coconut Salad
Crème Caramel With	
Poached Pears	Palm Sugar Sago Pudding

Menu 4

Mini Ulundu Vadais	Meat Pancake Rolls
Kofta Curry	Chettinad Chicken
Prawn Curry	Tomato Curry
Spiced Chickpea Curry	
With Potatoes	Eggplant And Yoghurt Salad
Fresh Tomato Salsa	Yellow Rice
Passion Fruit Cheese Cake	Pani Pol Pancakes

Glossary

Besan Flour (Indian)
Flour made from chickpeas used as a thickener for making certain vegetarian entrée dishes such as Pakorahs and Bondas.

Cardamoms
An aromatic seed used either whole or ground in sweet or savoury dishes for curries or cakes.

Cashew Nuts
A nut used both raw and roasted in Sri Lankan cooking.

Chow Chow
A mixture of preserved fruits and vegetables made in a heavy sugar and ginger syrup and used for Christmas Cake.

Chillies
Chilli is a spicy fruit that comes from a plant. It comes in many colours and sizes and the taste varies from mild to hot. Green chillies are used whole or sliced in curries, ground in chutneys, rice dishes and soups. Red chillies are used the same way, but also dried and crushed to make chilli flakes. It can also be ground into powder, which is available in Indian and Sri Lankan supermarkets.

Cumin
This spice blends beautifully with other spices and is essential in curries. It has a bitter taste but is extremely aromatic. It is also used in many rice dishes.

Cloves
Cloves are flower buds of a tree similar to Myrtle. It originated from the Spice Islands in Indonesia. These buds are picked twice a year and dried on mats in the sun. Cloves somewhat resemble a nail. Cloves have an intense flavour and can be fiery.

Curry Leaves
Small aromatic leaves from native tree used in curries to give the dish a pungent flavour. Crush it or chop into small pieces for more flavour.

Cinnamon Sticks

This spice comes from a bushy tree which, after a few years, is up-rooted and goes through a humidity process to dry out. The tree is then peeled and left to dry again in the sun before it is rolled by hand to produce quills or sticks. The best quality is grown in Sri Lanka and other parts of Asia.

Coriander Leaves

The aromatic fresh leaves of the coriander plant are both a herb and a garnish, and are used in Indian rice dishes, chutneys and curries. Coriander roots and stalks can also be minced and be used in curry dishes and soups.

Drumsticks (Murungai)

This is a slender nutritious tree grown in dry zones. The fruit of the tree has long thin pod resembling a drumstick and it is has a slight taste similar to asparagus. The leaves are used in many dishes in my cookbook, such as the Pittu and Crab Curry and can be bought in Indian and Sri Lankan spice shops in your city.

Dry Fish or Salted Fish

Many different types of fresh and salt-water fishes are salted and cured for general use in many South East Asian countries. Some are dried in the sun, some preserved in salt or brine. It has an acquired taste, it smells so pungent, and many people may disagree. Salted fish can be eaten with rice or used as a seasoning for vegetables, casseroles and meat dishes.

Fennel

Fennel is a herb with a flavour similar to Anise. It is widely grown in India and the Mediterranean and is a part of the parsley family. It is also available as a vegetable. It can be used in salads and stews.

Fenugreek Seeds

Fenugreek seeds grown on a Fenugreek plant. The dried seeds are used in fish dishes in my cookbook. It has a rich burnt sugar aroma.

Glossary

Garam Masala
Garam Masala is a spice mixture used to flavour curries, and as a condiment. I have included a recipe in my cookbook. It is very important to keep it fresh by storing in an airtight jar.

Ghee
Ghee is clarified butter. It gives a rich flavour to many recipes in my cookbook. It is also used in desserts and Indian sweets. Ghee is available in supermarkets and Asian spice shops. Once opened, it can be kept in the fridge for three months.

Garlic
Garlic is a bulb from the onion family and is used all over the world. Not only it is flavoursome, but also has great health-promoting properties. There are many varieties, some have very large cloves and are purple in colour, and some white.

Ginger
Ginger is a tuber that is consumed as a spice. Fresh root ginger has a refreshing scent and a sharp flavour. It is best bought fresh; it is available dry, but tastes different. It is a vital ingredient in Asian cooking. It should always be peeled before use and stored in the refrigerator or in a cool place in the kitchen.

Goraka (Gamboge)
Goraka (gamboge) is a bright orange fruit that is segmented and has a tangy taste. It grows mainly in India and Sri Lanka. It is dried in the sun and therefore turns black in colour. This fruit is mainly used in fish dishes. It is either ground fresh or it can be bought in a powder form. It must be used sparingly as it can be over-powering. It is also a substitute for tamarind and lime in certain dishes. In my cookbook, goraka (gamboge) is used for the preparation of the hot and sour dishes Miris Mallu and Ambul Thial.

Jackfruit
This fruit is shaped like a melon and similar in texture, with a greenish-yellow skin and little spikes. It grows to an enormous size and when young can be used as a vegetable (polos). When ripe it is a fruit. It is available at supermarkets and is exported from Asian countries.

Lemongrass (Serai)

Lemongrass is an aromatic leafy herb. The lower part is finely chopped or sliced and used in curries and is best when bought fresh. It is also available in powder and dried stalks.

Maldives Fish

Maldives Fish is cured Tuna Fish, produced in the Maldive Islands. It is widely used in Sri Lankan cuisine and known as Umbalakada in Sinhala and Marci in Tamil. The Tuna Fish is processed by boiling, smoking and sun-drying until it acquires a woody like appearance. It can be kept without refrigeration, for many months.

Mustard (Black)

This variety of mustard is smaller and stronger in taste than the yellow mustard variety.

Mint

Mint is an herb and the rounded leaf is used in cooking. It adds flavour to curries, chutneys and sambals, and is an important ingredient when making Korma, Biriyani and dipping sauces.

Nutmeg

This spice is very strong in flavour and used sparingly in desserts and cakes. It is always finely grated before using.

Palm Sugar (Jaggery)

This strong flavoured dark brown sugar comes from the sap of the coconut palm and Palmyrah palms. It is cooked until it crystallises and is packed in a round cake or cylinder form, and has a distinctive flavour.

Glossary

Palmyrah Root Flour
Palmyrah Root Flour comes from a perennial crop like coconut. These fruits are dried and the flour is used for making the soup Kool.

Pepper
Pepper is grown on the Piper Nigrum tree. The tree has green berries which, when dried, become black peppercorns.

Rampé (Pandan)
This is an aromatic leafy bush, bright green in colour, and beautiful and flavoursome in curries and rice dishes. It is used only very sparingly as its flavour can be over-powering. It only requires a little amount in a dish for flavour.

Spanish Saffron
Saffron is a spice derived from the stigma of the flower Saffron Crocus. The stalks connecting to the stigma are dried and are used in cooking as a seasoning agent. It gives a rich golden colour to food and is considered to be the world's most expensive spice you can buy.

Semolina
This is a product made from wheat. It is sold in either a medium grain or fine grain. It is used in cakes and sweets, and some savoury dishes.

Tamarind

Tamarind is a dark brown fruit in a pod, enclosed in a brittle shell, the size of a green bean. The flavour is sweet and sour and is used in many fish, meat and vegetable dishes, pickles and chutneys. In its dried form, with the seed removed, warm water is added to make a concentrated pulp and this is used in many recipes in my cookbook.

Turmeric

This is a tuber from the ginger family. The root is ground for use as a spice. It has a bitter flavour and a strong yellow hue and has to be used sparingly. It adds richness to dishes such as chilli potatoes and yellow rice and is widely used in many curry dishes.

Tandoori Mix

This is a spice blend of chillies, turmeric, cardamom, Garam Masala and saffron. See my recipe for Garam Masala and follow the recipe for Tandoori dishes.

Winter Melon (Dong Gua)

Pumpkin preserve is made with this fruit. This fruit is prepared the same way as a pumpkin. The rind is cut off and the seeds are discarded and the fibre is scooped from the centre before you cut into strips, cubes or wedges, to prepare a pumpkin preserve. Chinese super-markets, open vegetable markets carry this fruit. It can be used in savoury dishes as well as dessert.

Measures And Conversions

1 cup almond meal	3¾ oz	110 g
1 cup caster sugar	7 oz	220 g
1 cup icing sugar	5 oz	150 g
1 cup plain or self-raising flour	5 oz	150 g
1 cup white sugar	7 oz	220 g

Cup Conversions ~ Solid Measures

Metric	Imperial
20 g	¾ oz
60 g	2 oz
125 g	4 oz
180 g	6 oz
250 g	8 oz
500 g	16 oz (1 lb)
1 kg	32 oz (2 lb)

Cup Conversions ~ Liquid Measures

Cups	Metric	Imperial
⅓ cup	80 ml	2 ½ fl oz
½ cup	125 ml	4 fl oz
⅔ cup	160 ml	5 fl oz
¾ cup	180 ml	6 fl oz
1 cup	250 ml	8 fl oz
2 cups	500 ml	16 fl oz (1 American pint)
2½ cups	625 ml	20 fl oz (1 Imperial pint)
4 cups	1 litre	32 fl oz

Oven Temperature

Gas Mark	C	F
2	150°c	300°f
3	170°c	325°f
4	180°c	350°f
6	200°c	400°f
7	220°c	425°f

Cooking Tips

Appetizers, Snacks And Salads

Remember that all leafy green vegetables are very delicate, and should be cooked for a minute only, to preserve all of the vitamins and minerals.

Spices, Mixtures And Curry Pastes

To release more flavour from cinnamon, grill the quills before adding to the curry to bring out the aromatic smells.

Bruise lemongrass for more pungent flavour before adding to the recipe.
Adjust the amount of chillies added to the recipe for a milder taste.

Vegetable Curries

Tearing curry leaves into a curry will give them a pungent smell and enhance the flavour!

Do not boil the coconut milk used in your curries for too long. This prevents it from separating.

For garnishing, deep-fried drumstick leaves, continental parsley or any other herbs provide a nice decoration with their fragile crispy texture.

Potatoes

For cooking, baking or making sweets select the right type of potatoes. Pontiacs are of smooth texture and are good for baking, frying, and boiling. Golden Delights (unwashed potatoes) are good for mash, and roasting.

Fish And Shellfish

Do not overcook seafood. Once the sauce is brought to the boil, seafood such as prawns and squid take only a minute or two to cook. If cooked for longer, it tends to turn rubbery. Fish takes about four minutes to cook after you bring the sauce to the boil.

When buying prawns, always look for fresh ones with shiny eyes, thick shells and the head intact.

For the best results when deep-frying fish, make sure the oil is hot when you put the fish in, so the outside of the fish cooks evenly and becomes crispy, and then reduce to medium heat to cook fish through.

Meat And Poultry

Marinate meat for at least two hours in the refrigerator with the mixture of spices and salt, and follow the recipe. Be sure to use a glass or ceramic dish if your marinade consists of citrus juice, vinegar or garlic, as the acid may react with metal utensils and taint the food.